INSIDE KNOWLEDGE

How Women Can Thrive in Professional Service Firms

INSIDE KNOWLEDGE

How Women Can Thrive in Professional Service Firms

BY

ALISON TEMPERLEY

United Kingdom – North America – Japan
India – Malaysia – China

Emerald Publishing Limited
Howard House, Wagon Lane, Bingley BD16 1WA, UK

First edition 2017

Reprints and permissions service
Contact: permissions@emeraldinsight.com

British Library Cataloguing in Publication Data
A catalogue record for this book is available from the British Library

ISBN: 978-1-78714-566-5 (Print)
ISBN: 978-1-78714-565-8 (Online)
ISBN: 978-1-78714-977-9 (Epub)

Printed and bound by CPI Group (UK) Ltd, Croydon, CR0 4YY

ISOQAR certified
Management System,
awarded to Emerald
for adherence to
Environmental
standard
ISO 14001:2004.

ISOQAR
REGISTERED
Certificate Number 1985
ISO 14001

INVESTOR IN PEOPLE

To all the wonderful women who have contributed to this book in many different ways.

The secret of getting ahead is getting started. The secret of getting started is breaking your complex overwhelming tasks into small manageable tasks, and starting on the first one.

— Mark Twain

CONTENTS

Foreword   ix

Preface — Why You Need This Book   xv

1. An Analysis of the Uneven Playing Field   1

2. Why Should You Focus on Your Career Now?
   A Call to Be Conscious because You Are Important   9

3. Working to Get the Most Out of Your Time and
   Your Brain — Your Key Tools for Success   15

4. What Do You Offer Your Firm?   39

5. Are You Ambitious? If So What Are You
   Ambitious for?   45

6. Where Are You Starting from? Getting Feedback   63

7. Taking Stock   73

8. Impression Management — What Do You Do
   and How Do You Talk about It?   81

9.   Politics — How Do You Get Involved?   95

10.   Stepping Forward   105

11.   Who Knows What You Do — Effective and
      Efficient Networking   117

12.   Sponsorship: The Sharp End of Your
      Developmental Network   135

13.   Role Models   145

14.   Finding Your Equilibrium   151

15.   Being Commercial   163

16.   Developing Your Business   171

17.   Making the Most of Your Appraisals   183

18.   Preparing for Promotion Processes   193

Appendix: Questions from Promotion Panels   209

Wider Resources   215

About the Author   221

Index   223

FOREWORD

*By Claudia Parzani, Linklaters Regional
Managing Partner for Western Europe*

THE KITE

I was born in a small town where every dream seemed too big to come true.

I thought it was because I was still a child, with short pig-tails, a pink smock and a white bow. I laid the blame on my age. "I will grow up and certainly my dreams will find their own space then" — I thought — "small dreams for babies and big dreams for adults". But, after having waved goodbye to my school uniform with a smile, I understood that the blame was not on my age, but rather on the air, on the low sky that I breathed, on what I was told and taught at home and at school. My biggest dreams, those highest, most beautiful ones, those I would have liked to see flying like a magic kite high in the sky, would never find their air. Because I was a girl. Because the wind was not for me.

FOLLOWING THE WIND

I am not sure that I have been truly ambitious in my life, not enough according to my male friends anyway. I have never fought, not once, just for the pleasure of getting a position, a title or a role. However, I am sure that I have always been determined, determined to follow the wind and my dreams to their horizons, no matter what. Of course, while following the wind, I sometimes felt that I might fall, but I also felt, deep down in my heart, that I would always pick myself up again, perhaps not always stronger, but always with a lesson learned.

And so, following the wind, I left that small town where everyone knew each other's names, holding my head high while looking for broader horizons, for cities with a different air, for higher skies where my kite would fly in the wind.

Me, all on my own, with only one piece of luggage: my dreams. Those of the young girl I had been, those of the girl I was, and those of the woman that I would become.

TOUCHING THE SKY

Today I am a lawyer. I love my clients, the deals that I do, I warm in finding new solutions to old problems, in changing the expected order of things into dynamic, unexpected harmony. Every morning I go to work with a smile, and in the evening, on my way back home, I realize that I haven't lost it, that it's still there, just like the rainbow-colored kite that follows me around everywhere. I work for a firm that I love and that has proven to me time and again that it believes in women and their dreams.

But this is not enough for me. I have found the wind, I have learnt to fly high and yet I want more. Because for many years now, I wake up in the morning with the same wish burning deep inside of me, the desire to leave a better world to my three daughters, a world where women who reach important positions do not make it into the news, a world where merit is the rule and gender doesn't matter, a world where each kite can reach the wind and touch the sky.

YOU AND ME

That is why YOU are my biggest dream now! You are the generation of women that will change the sky above our firms, above our society, above each and every country in this world.

You are the ones born with the wind in your hair and today's young girls will look at you and believe that everything is really possible, that the world truly belongs to all of us, that passion, energy and commitment can truly transform every single dream we dream into reality. And that the air that we all breathe was really made for flying.

Our firms, our society and our world need You. We cannot throw away one-half of all the talent there is, we cannot renounce the ability to see the world with new and different eyes, we cannot afford to squander the chance to take better decisions every day.

That is why today I am here with Alison and with you.

You who have bought this book or have received it as a gift from someone who loves you and wants to support you — you must be ambitious.

You have to remember at every moment of your life you have all you need to get where you want to go within yourself.

You have to be aware that the limits before you are only reflections of your tired eyes, your dark thoughts and your fearful dreams. Take a breath and take courage, because you were born to fly.

Do not swap your personal life for your career; the wisdom needed for the realization of both such dreams is already inside you.

Do not wait for the right moment; there is no better moment than this one, the bravery to take a run-up and head into the wind is already inside you.

Do not ask for the impossible, the important thing is to start to fly, the wisdom needed to find your unique piece of sky is already inside you.

Raise your hand even when you doubt that you are the right person for the task. Most probably you are the right person for it; you just need to get over your fear of flying and admit to yourself that you want that position, that title or that project.

Raise your hand when the race is about to start, do not be afraid of losing. We all slip and fall down sometimes, but in order to win you have to run, to give it a try, to get closer to the starting blocks.

Raise your hand whenever someone is asking for help. Give to those who ask, never be greedy, never be envious.

Be truly a woman, proud of your style, authentic and sincere.

Be truly a woman but have fun as if you were still a young girl. Always try to be happy, cherish the small things and enjoy the many choices you have every day.

Be truly a woman, a brave woman, continue to follow your dreams with every single beat of your heart.

And if while following your path you encounter a hurdle and fall down, feeling that the strength to raise up is leaving you, please don't give up but look for a woman like Alison or me, a woman that will always believe that you are the most beautiful mirror that the sky can have. We will help you, because your pain is also our pain, your path is also our path, your dream is also our dream.

And now please hurry and read.

I am here waiting for you, here, under this huge sky, with the cord of my kite in my hands and with the sweet and warm wind in my hair.

PREFACE – WHY YOU NEED THIS BOOK

After all, Ginger Rogers did everything that Fred Astaire did. She just did it backwards and in high heels.

— Ann Richards

This book is written for you if you are an ambitious woman working in a professional services firm (accountants, lawyers or consultants) and are eager to achieve career success by maximising your potential in your firm. It is practical and comes from work with over a thousand women in professional service firms just like you. In this book I have brought together all the advice and practical exercises that these wonderful women have found useful – *Inside Knowledge.*

This book is called *Inside Knowledge* because it comes from what I, and the women I have worked with, have found out from inside professional service firms. The title also refers to gaining knowledge about yourself – knowledge of what you want and what you have the potential to achieve in the firm you work in.

Whilst there are commonalities, professional service firms are different from other commercial organisations. The partners who run the business also own it and consequently the political landscape is more complex.

Professional service firms sell the skills of their people, both partners and staff, and explicitly aim to be meritocracies. Many bright, high achieving women are drawn to such organisations because of the implicit promise that, as in academia, if you are clever and work hard you will fulfil your potential. But if that is your expectation you are apt to find the reality of what goes on in a professional service firm is more complicated than you supposed. It would also appear to be the case that in this challenging environment women are not faring as well as their male peers.

If you look at the graduate intake of most professional service firms, 50% of the intake is female. If you look at the partner population, typically around 20% of the equity partners are female. Partnership is not the only measure of success and it may not be yours; however, these percentages are indicative of what is happening to women in professional service firms and of how both you and your firm lose out when your potential is not realised.

Over the past 30 years I have worked in and for professional service firms designing and running women's leadership programmes as well as coaching women and men at all levels. My experience has been that the women I work with do excellent work but often fail to actively manage their careers; to do the things, beyond the excellent work, that get you noticed, sponsored and promoted. I am often asked if I have written a book so that the women I work with can pass on the tips, tools and advice that have been honed by many years of working with more than a thousand women in professional service firms from around the world. This is that book.

WHERE THIS BOOK COMES FROM — MY PERSONAL STORY

On 28 August 1984, I started work at Coopers & Lybrand (a precursor of PwC) at a residential course for new graduates in Manchester. As we stood at Manchester Piccadilly station waiting to be picked up we all looked cautiously at each other wondering where this career would take us.

Every year similar cohorts are assembling all over the world just as we did. Much has happened in the meantime, not least in people's expectations. The young women starting now were not even born when I stood on that station, but still their chances of their careers taking them to partnership remain remote. This book passes on all the tips I have accumulated, not only in my 17 years of working for PwC, but also in my decade of designing and running women's leadership programmes internationally and coaching women and men in professional service firms around the globe.

I remember one of our partners at that opening residential programme in Manchester asking us to look to the person to our right and then to look at the person on our left and then to understand that only one of us would be with the firm after the first 3 years of training. I made it through the training and rose through the ranks to run my own teams and a large client base before being lured into coaching, training and development.

I have run my own business as a coach working for professional service firms for 16 years, almost as long as I worked for PwC. I have loved my work inside PwC and outside it. I have worked with remarkable people across the world and seen my coachees flourish and grow, fulfilling their potential and making me very proud of their successes.

I wish I had known in 1984 what I know now, and that is my aim; to give you all the inside knowledge I have gained for myself and from others so that you have all the information, tools, techniques and skills that I have seen being useful as a woman in a professional service firm.

HOW TO USE THIS BOOK

The book is divided into 18 chapters. Each chapter focuses on a subject that women like you have found helpful to examine and work on. The chapters do build on each other but are designed so that you can pick up each one separately if that is more useful for you.

Chapter 1 analyses the context within which you work, the current preponderance of male partners and the interlinking individual, organisational and societal contributors to this slued partner population

If you are a 'pick and dip' reader rather than a 'start from the beginning and work your way through' reader, can I suggest you read Chapters 2 and 3 before you start as they give you some of the key information on why you should focus on your career now. They also set out the tools that underlie both your engagement with your career and the subject matter of every subsequent chapter.

The following chapters come in complementary pairs (mostly).

Chapters 4 and 5 are companions as Chapter 4 gets you to think about what you offer before Chapter 5 helps you explore what you want to get from that offering.

Similarly, Chapters 6 and 7 should be read together as they are about understanding where you are now. Firstly, by assessing the feedback that you have from others and then by bringing that together with all your other knowledge to take stock of your strengths, weaknesses, opportunities and threats.

Chapters 8 and 9 look at what you want others to say about you before we meet the political players in our world and examine the usefulness of politics. As a spoiler my conclusion is that politics is value neutral, it is just a fact of life, it is how you play it and to what end that is the real choice.

Chapters 10 and 11 are about your interaction with the outside world. Stepping forward to engage and engaging efficiently and effectively by networking.

Chapters 12 and 13 look at the importance of your development network and particularly your sponsor and how you choose your role models. Chapter 13 is particularly poignant for me as one of the key factors in me leaving PwC was what I perceived to be the lack of role models. I wish I had had the knowledge then that I do now, this chapter would have been particularly useful.

Chapter 14 stands alone. It is about finding a sustainable equilibrium that works for you, making room in the 24/7 that you have available to you for your career and all the other things you want in your life.

Chapters 15 and 16 are vital (I would say that as I am a chartered accountant). They look at your place in the firm. Your firm is a business and needs to make money, your skills are what the firm sells. It is important that you are aware of the business benefits of what you contribute and how you can increase those benefits by building your business.

Chapters 17 and 18 look at how you engage with the firm during appraisal and promotion processes so that you are prepared and can show others what you are really capable of.

In each case the chapters have exercises that look simple but which women I have worked with have found both difficult and extremely helpful. Those women would echo my plea for you to write on this book, do the exercises as they will make the learning real and specific to you.

At the end of every chapter there is a section where I challenge you to do something different, to take action. I have also included the tips that partners have given women I have worked with over the years in women's leadership programmes. I hope these will inform and inspire you to do something different or to think about things differently.

The Appendix sets out questions from promotion panels in professional service firms. I have collected these over the years from men and women I have worked with.

WHY FOCUS ON THE WOMEN?

The women I have worked with are exceptionally bright, creative, self-aware and fun. So are the men. However, the statistics suggest there are things that hold women back when compared with their male peers and this book focuses on what we women can do about that. What it does not do is seek to minimise the firms' part in the failure of women to get to the top. Nor do I wish to ignore the wonderful things that women bring to their work. Perhaps that is my next job, to write a companion volume for partners in professional service firms setting out their part in this imbalance together with a book for all setting out the fabulous attributes women contribute to their firms. In the meantime, it is important for you to gain awareness of the value you bring to your firm, what might be holding you back and what you can do about it.

GENERALISATIONS AND GEOGRAPHY

In writing this book I have had to resort to generalisations to make the language flow, but of course I do realise that not all women think and behave in the same way and the same is true for men. Indeed there are many more similarities than there are differences. The research suggests that there are however ways in which women tend to behave and I have used those generalisations as a learning tool. They may or may not apply to you, but I hope discussing them helps you think about how you do things.

I am also aware of the many different cultural overlays that inform who we are and how we work. The research in this field is largely based on studies carried out in the West and in particular from the United States and the United Kingdom. This is a shame and I know people are working hard gathering and analysing data from other cultures. In this book I have only used the data that women I have worked with have found useful whatever their culture. It is also worth noting that if you work for an international firm the culture of the firm will also influence the culture of the office.

I understand that in a well-cut diamond all the faces look into the core of the diamond. In the same way there are many ways to look into and understand you and the ways that you operate at work. Your actions can be usefully examined with reference to your culture, your age, your psychological make-up and your gender. This book concentrates on the latter but other ways of looking at you are no less valid.

FROM ME TO YOU

The book is designed with you in mind; I do hope you find it helpful. I want you to succeed and fulfil your potential in whatever way is important to you.

CHAPTER 1

AN ANALYSIS OF THE UNEVEN PLAYING FIELD

If we use the analogy of the playing field as the arena we enter as we start our careers in professional service firms, is there a tilt in that field which means that the advantages naturally flow more easily towards the male players?

After one of the women's leadership programmes I ran for a professional service firm, two of the participants ran sessions for their teams on what they had learned from the programme. A number of the other women in the team thanked them profusely saying that the tools and tips were insightful, helpful and new — they had not thought about the firm and their place in it in that way before. A few men also gave their feedback to the presenters; they felt that the session was just setting out what they saw as obvious political reality. Why was there this difference in how the men and women viewed the context in which they work? What inside knowledge had the men already gained?

I do not believe that the answer to creating a level playing field is requiring women to do things differently, to simply 'lean in', work harder or behave more like a man. All the work I do also includes working with the professional service firm to ensure that the espoused meritocracy is enacted. Simply 'fixing the women' is neither attractive nor does it work, in that it overlooks at least half of the contributing factors. However, there are things that we, as women within professional service firms, can do authentically to ensure that what we do is given the weight it deserves — and that is what this book is designed to help you do.

WHY SO FEW FEMALE PARTNERS?

In 2013 and 2015 McKinsey did some work for the 30% Club in the United Kingdom, interviewing, reviewing data and surveying many of the United Kingdom's leading professional service firms (McKinsey & 30% Club Reports, 2012, 2015). Their conclusion was that on their first day at work a man starting in a law firm in 2015 was three times as likely to become a partner as the woman standing next to him. This meant that law firms had caught up with the accountancy and consulting firms whose men were reported as being three times more likely to make partner than their female peers in the earlier report.

Brilliance is not the only requirement for partnership. You need to have a strong business case and excellent personal skills; however, there are things that you can do to put yourself in the best position to fulfil your potential and achieve the career success you want.

Before we concentrate on what women can take control of in the rest of this book, let us challenge some of the 'obvious' but questionable reasons given for why women do not make it to the top in equal numbers in firms that pride themselves on being meritocracies.

It could be that women are leaving when they have babies and do not return to work because they want to spend all their time with their growing children or desire to take on less challenging roles when they do return and any ambition to progress is left behind in the delivery room. This is certainly an anecdotally attractive explanation. However, in a study sponsored by EY, Goldman Sachs and Lehman Brothers, the Centre for Work-Life Policy interviewed a large number of highly educated women in the United States who had left paid employment and found that 93% wanted to return after a break to have children or look after elders (Hewlett & Luce, 2005). This challenges the assumption that those who have commitments outside work which take them away for relatively short periods of their careers will not want to return or will want to take a less ambitious 'mommy track' for the rest of their careers. It will be true for some but not for all. It is also worth pointing out that not all women either want to or can have children.

It could be that professional service firms' traditional business model inadvertently discriminates against women. This model requires potential partners to be working towards partnership in their thirties, precisely the time when women who are mothers are experiencing the most demanding years of motherhood. I do believe that this is a contributing factor, but it is not the whole story.

It could be that women are simply not as bright; however, almost nobody would defend that position today, although it was a widely held belief as recently as a century ago.

It could be that women do not actively manage their careers in the way that many men do and firms implicitly expect. My experience suggests that this is certainly a contributing factor to the lack of women at the top of professional service firms. It is this that you can influence. This book is designed to show you the things that can help you ensure that you actively manage your career so that it gives you what you want and deserve.

THE INDIVIDUAL VERSUS THE ORGANISATION VERSUS SOCIETY

I love Sheryl Sandberg's book *Lean In* (Sandberg, 2013), but the implicit instruction in the title tells only part of the story. Sandberg and I agree, there are things that we can do as women to 'Lean In' and the book you are reading is designed as a practical guide to help you do this in professional service firms. However, this is not enough — the organisations you work for also need to change.

Most managing partners see the business case that underlies the need for change. They recognise that their existing and potential clients want their advisors to reflect their values and diversity and regard firms that field homogenous teams as old fashioned. They also see that the female talent inside and outside the firm wants to know what is being done to ensure the career playing field is level. After all, who would choose to pursue their career in a place where they believe they will be disadvantaged because they are a woman?

Against this push for equality is the opposing weight of individual unconscious bias and a career structure built for men in the last century (if not the century before). To give but one example, there is unconscious bias in the widely held desire for potential partners to have 'gravitas,' a word derived from the Latin for weight or heaviness and often associated with large physical forms and deep voices. I would suggest gravitas is a description predicated on traditionally male attributes. Unconscious bias in both the systemic processes and the plethora of individual decisions needs to be addressed to create a level playing field.

However, it is not just our firms that are designed on a male model; our societies have been built to support men in the workplace and women still do the majority of the home and child care in almost all societies.

Whilst I have strong views about the systems at play in organisations and the wider society that will have to change in order for true meritocracy to flourish, this book is about you and what is within your own power. I accept that this is only part of the story, but it is the part you can most easily affect.

Much of what I have written in this book is good advice for all who work in professional service firms; it is not that women are particularly remedial in any of these aspects, but the bare facts suggest that women are not getting the career advancement that their skills would suggest we should expect. I would propose that part of this is that women are not as well sponsored as their male colleagues. There is a very human tendency to advise and support people that remind us of our younger selves. Whilst less than a fifth of partners are female, women are not getting the detailed sponsorship that their male peers are benefiting from.

This book is what a good sponsor should tell you early on in your career and keep reminding you of as you progress.

The only thing that is within your power to change is the way you think and behave, but that is a powerful tool in changing the reactions and relationships you have in the firm around you. I am asking you to be aware of the consequences of your actions and to consider flexing them consciously to help yourself and others.

Tips from the top — Advice from partners to women in their firm

'In the past women tried to be like men, then they tried to be superwomen, now they are being normal women, and expecting the firm to help them. That makes this a good time to be a woman in a professional service firm'.

RESOURCES

McKinsey & 30% Club Reports (2012). *Shifting the needle.*

McKinsey & 30% Club Reports (2015). *The needle starts to shift.*

Hewlett, S. A., & Luce, C. B. (2005). Off-ramps and on-ramps: Keeping talented women on the road to success. *Harvard Business Review*, 83(3), 43–46, 48, 50–54.

Sandberg, S. (2013). *Lean In: Women work and the will to lead.* New York, NY: WH Allen.

CHAPTER 2

WHY SHOULD YOU FOCUS ON YOUR CAREER NOW? A CALL TO BE CONSCIOUS BECAUSE YOU ARE IMPORTANT

If you always do what you have always done you will always get what you have always gotten
— Henry Ford

As human beings we do not embrace change unless we are benefitted from that change. Doing things differently requires effort; it is much easier to continue in patterns that have been successful for us in the past. Many women in professional service firms have been extremely successful in their past academic work. The pattern embedded from school and university is that you do brilliant work, somebody marks it objectively and you move forward in the system. The kind of people you are working with now are very similar to those you were with at university and now, like then, the quality of your brain and its ability to acquire knowledge, understand and analyse information is a vital element in the work and your success. The difference is that in your career post university this brainpower is necessary but no longer sufficient for the system to recognise and reward you. You have to take an active role in your career beyond the work you do to fulfil your potential and achieve what you want.

The good news is that you can really make a difference to your career success by being aware and working smarter, not harder. The bad news is that you will have to step outside your comfort zone and do some things differently to make things happen.

WHAT IS IN IT FOR ME?

So what are the good things that might make you want to try out some changes now? These might include a range from the following:

- Building the future life that you want both inside and outside of work

- Working on the most interesting client projects

- Expanding your knowledge and experience by working for a wider range of partners and clients

- Realising your potential and achieving the promotions you deserve within the firm

- Maximising your influence in the team and the organisation so that the changes you believe in are executed

- Maximising your earning power

- Building your CV for a future move outside the firm

If none of these are important to you then you may not need to examine the way you do things, but if they are important then it is worth being conscious about what you are doing and the consequent results. It is worth noting that doing nothing different is a valid choice if it is conscious. My concern is about those who do not think about what they are doing and thus make no changes.

If you do decide to do something different as a result of this book the time to make changes is now; a delay is merely putting back the time when you get what you want and delayed gratification is over rated. You may need to establish new patterns of behaviour which will take time, focus and practice and the sooner you start the sooner they will become 'second nature'.

AUTHENTICITY

I am not asking you to change who you are or behave like a different person or a different gender, but we change throughout life as we learn strategies that are more effective for us, while retaining the values that are fundamental to us. I am not asking you to change who you are or to behave inauthentically; I believe we all have an authentic range, we do not behave exactly the same way with all our friends, family and strangers, rather we flex our behaviour within our range. The change I am talking about involves you flexing your style, not twisting it out of shape.

HOW WE LEARN

Learning new ways of operating requires time and effort.

Before we first try something out we are often unconsciously incompetent; think how you viewed driving a car before you took your first lesson. I certainly had no idea how incompetent I would be, it looked easy. Once you get into the car for your first lesson you become consciously aware that you are incompetent and you need lessons before you become consciously competent. At this stage I remember having to remind myself, 'mirror, signal, manoeuvre' before making any move. Practice brings round unconscious competence when you do things automatically. The danger is that these patterns become so automatic that they can tip into incompetence without us noticing and the circle begins again (**Figure 2.1**).

Figure 2.1:   The Process of Learning.

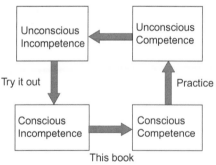

Taking responsibility for your career and addressing the elements I will cover in this book will take you through the same learning cycle. You may not have considered what could be holding you back and be in unconscious incompetence; alternatively, you may realise you are not addressing aspects of how you move forward and are not sure what to do (conscious incompetence). In either case, my intent is to help you get to conscious competence so that all you need to do is practice. Trying out new things will start by feeling 'awkward' and 'unnatural' (rather like the 'mirror, signal, manoeuvre' stage in learning to drive) but with practice it will become the natural way that you operate without thought.

My Challenges to You

1. Think about what you want to get from this book. Is it a reference book or a 'virtual' programme? What do you need from it at this stage in your career?

2. Decide how you are going to engage with this book and what you need to do to help you do that. Are you going to:

   - skim read it all and then focus on a chapter a week depending on what you have coming up in your diary and the relevance of the chapter; or

   - read a chapter a week in the order I have set out; or

   - read the chapters that you think you need help on now and use it like a reference book to help with challenges as they arise; or

   - read it alongside one of your colleagues and discuss your views on each chapter?

You may want to actively take on the challenges I set for you at the end of every chapter. Alternatively, you may wish to use it more passively as a prompt to make you more conscious so that you can observe and learn from those around you.

3. Doing the exercises will make what I am talking about more personal and helpful to you and your career. This is a book I suggest you write on, answer the questions and please use the margins to make your notes and make the book your own resource of my thoughts and yours.

For those who want to explore further I have suggested resources after every chapter and in the back of the book.

Tips from the top — Advice from partners to women in their firm

'Know yourself well and be yourself, the best version of yourself'.

'You may not have all the answers now, but you will find a way if you want to succeed'.

'There are three 'C's of partnership

- Choice — you are an adult making a choice, not a sacrifice.

- Challenge — this is never going to be easy, and that is part of the fun of it.

- Committed — you need to drive your career'.

CHAPTER 3

WORKING TO GET THE MOST OUT OF YOUR TIME AND YOUR BRAIN — YOUR KEY TOOLS FOR SUCCESS

Time abides long enough for those who make use of it

— Leonardo da Vinci

Working in a professional service firm involves long hours and demanding clients. It is easy to feel caught between the conflicting demands of clients, partners, colleagues and life at home. How do you get the most for you, as well as the firm, from the limited resources of a 24-hour day and a human brain?

The following is a checklist — my suggestion is that you review the list and then use it as a prompt to garner the help that is available, from within you, within the firm and from your network. None of the items on the list are revolutionary and you may well have thought about doing them already, but have you actually changed your habits so that you do get the benefit?

My checklist:

1. How to get the most from your focus

2. How to get the most from your energy

3. How you can get the most from your time

4. How do you get the most from others

5. How to get the most from your mental capacity

In the remainder of this chapter I will explore each of these in turn; in each case, giving you the tools that other women like you have found useful.

HOW TO GET THE MOST FROM YOUR FOCUS

Your 'To Do' List

Most of us in professional service firms are driven by our 'to do' lists. These inspire and at times depress us, but they always exert some level of control over us. They are designed to help us focus our limited time and brain space on what is important.

Is working on your career on your 'to do' list? Do you make good quality time available for planning your career? If not, why not? Is this because you do not think it is important? If you yourself do not give your career and ambitions time and attention then you cannot expect others to do so.

Stephen Covey in his book *Seven Habits of Highly Successful People* (Covey, 2004) introduced a really useful model which I suggest you may wish to employ to structure your 'to do' list. Most of us write a vertical list using bullet points, but a more useful way to set them out is using Covey's four box model (**Figure** 3.1):

Figure 3.1: Stephen Covey's Four Box Model.

	Urgent	Not Urgent
Important	1	2
Not important	3	4

Source: Covey (2004).

We all recognise the need to do the items listed in Box 1 first, but for many of us there is an urge to do the urgent but not important things, Box 3, second rather than the important, but not urgent matters in Box 2. Considering your career and many of the topics covered in the following chapters should be in the important but not urgent box and are easily overlooked if you always deal with the urgent items first.

If items are not important you may wish to consider delegating or not doing them to make time for the important items. If the parameters that separate important and not important in your work tasks are not clear to you, this is a useful discussion to have with those that you work with. I would suggest your career is always in the important boxes and always part of your focus.

Exercise
Here is a blank box for you to play with. I suggest you put your current 'to do' list in these four boxes to help

you ensure you are focussing on the things that are really important to you.

	Urgent	Not urgent
Important		
Not important		

Make sure your career development is in one of the important boxes — because it is.

Your Development File

In order to make it easy to focus on your career I suggest you ensure that all the information about your development and your career are kept in a place that they can be easily found and updated. I suggest you have a file (electronic or paper) that contains:

- The feedback you have been given over the last 5 years

- Copies of the appraisals you have had over the last 5 years

- Other developmental reports from courses

- Your CV and any biographies of you that are used by the firm

- A draft of the appraisal form you will have to fill in at the end of the year so that you can add to it during the year while things are still at the front of your mind

- A draft of the papers you will need to submit for your next promotion (if such papers exist) so that you know what you will need and can plan to be ready.

HOW TO GET THE MOST FROM YOUR ENERGY

There is not an exact correlation between the hours we put into work and the way we feel about that work. What makes a good day good is often not the number of hours we put in, but the relationship between the energy we put into and get from what we do during the day.

In our daily lives there are activities that give us energy and those that drain energy.

Exercise

Start compiling a list of what activities give you energy, and what drains it. Some activities are obvious and will be easy to identify, others will not occur to you immediately. My suggestion is to keep the list open and add to it over the next few days as other activities occur to you, both as energy boosters and drains.

What drains your energy?   What gives you energy?

Energy givers might be particular aspects of your work, working with particular people, learning new things inside or outside work, exercise, meeting friends, getting out of the office at lunch time, eating properly or coaching juniors. It is worth noticing how often we surrender some of these things first when we are under pressure, with the result that we gain a few more minutes but lose energy and focus, thus counterbalancing any small gain in time.

Exercise

Once you have identified what gives you more energy, how can you do more of these things?

What gives me energy?	How can I do more of this?

(Continued)

What gives me energy?	How can I do more of this?

It is also worth being very clear with yourself about what drains your energy. Again some aspects of your work might be a drain, so might working with particular people. Explore what drains your energy outside work. For some people routine admin is a joy and for others it is a drain — what drains you? Some energy drains are unavoidable, others are the result of bad planning and poor delegation. It is worth identifying what it is that drains your energy and how you and others have minimised the impact of the energy drain.

Exercise

Once you have identified what drains your energy, how can you do less of these things?

What drains my energy?	How can I do less of this?

HOW YOU CAN GET THE MOST FROM YOUR TIME

Your diary is a vital tool. Take control of it. If you do not use it for what you want, work will find its way into all of the uncontrolled spaces. My suggestion is that you consider which of the tips I set out below would work for you and then you put them in your diary as a regular, recurring appointment to hold back the tide of work. That may not be possible this week or this month due to existing commitments, but look at your diary for the rest of the year — when can you put such regular weekly or monthly appointments in? If, when you get to the appointment, you are very busy and decide to take the diary entry out, you are doing this consciously and aware of the consequences to your energy and strategic thought. If the slots are not put in now well in advance you will never find the time to insert them later.

Here are three practical tips that you might find useful:

Find Energy Boosting Slots in Your Diary

I know you are very busy, and you have identified the things that give you energy, but how do you get the time to do the energy boosters? There are three key slots in the pattern of a normal working day that you could use very productively, but which many people allow work to seep into and therefore lose. It is worth identifying them, protecting them and then using them.

The first slot is before you get into work. Could you use that time more helpfully to give you energy? Is this a time to go to an exercise class, walk part of the way to work, or meet somebody for breakfast? I am not suggesting that you do this every day, but it is worth considering protecting time to do something that gives you energy before you get into work at least once a week. If you want to try it, put it into your diary as a regular recurring appointment.

The second slot is during your lunch break. You know that eating lunch at your desk or not eating it at all is not good for your body or the physical organ that is your brain, so my suggestion is that you take control of the lunch time slot and make some appointments that will give you energy for the afternoon and for the rest of the week. Go out of the office to get lunch so that your mind and body have something else to do, meet somebody for lunch, do some exercise or plan something that makes you happy. Put it in your diary as a recurring weekly slot. You can take it out nearer the time if you really need to, but only if you can justify that removal to yourself.

The most difficult slot to preserve is the one at the end of the day. The temptation to 'just get this done' is huge, but remember how much better your brain is first thing in the morning, what takes you a long time tonight will take you much less time in the morning. Regular, recurring slots for exercise, socialising and fun are good for you, but you need to make them and protect them. Often the person you need to protect them from is you.

Exercise

Review the shape of your normal working week. There are three potential energy boosting slots a day and 5 days in a working week, which makes 15 energy boosting slots available to you. Which ones are you going to use and what for?

	Monday	Tuesday	Wednesday	Thursday	Friday
Before work					
Lunch time					
After work					

If you want to use them they need to be booked out in your diary on a recurring and regular basis.

Put in Recurring Time to Think and Plan

For example, why don't you put in time to review your career every month for the rest of the year? If you do not put it in now you will never find the time as other projects will squeeze the time from your diary. You would do this for an important client project, so you should do it for this key personal project.

My suggestion is that you schedule a 'meeting' with MS on the first hour of the first Tuesday of every month. MS stands for myself. If Monday is always madly busy, then Tuesday is a good day to plan; find the day and time that works for your work pattern.

The rules of this 'meeting' are as follows.

— This is not time to 'do', this is time to strategically plan and think.

— You do not work at your desk — find a meeting room or a café on the way to work so that you will not be disturbed.

— You do not work on, or even read, your emails — switch off the internet for the hour of the 'meeting' so that you have peace to really think.

— Have in front of you only your diary, your 'to do' list, your development file (see above) and the equivalent of a clean sheet of paper (electronic or real).

— You spend the first 20 minutes looking back by doing the following:

  ○ Identifying your achievements over the last month

  ○ Updating your internal biographies, CV and client database as appropriate to reflect these before they are forgotten in the passage of time

  ○ Planning how those who would find it useful to be told formally of what you have achieved will get to know the facts so they are making decisions with easy access to that data.

— You spend the remaining 40 minutes looking forward:

  ○ What have you got coming up in the next month? Review your 'to do' list and your diary.

- What is really important coming up? Differentiate the important from the urgent but not important.

- Strategically what do you need to do to be in a good position to tackle the challenges?

- How are you going to manage your diary so that you get enough of the things that give you energy and minimise the impact of the things that will drain your energy?

- What can you delegate and to whom?

- Who can support you in what you are aiming to accomplish?

- How are you doing against the criteria you will be assessed on at the end of the year? Are there additional actions you need to undertake to meet those criteria?

- What do you want from your career? What actions do you need to undertake in the next month to facilitate your career goals?

Use Your Diary as a Tool

You have to be very organised in your work in professional service firms and use your diary to manage and record your time accurately. I suggest you also use your diary as an active tool to prompt you to think about things that need attention but are not urgent. Perhaps a monthly prompt to think about business development or impression management will help you keep your focus on these important parts of your career management long after you have put this book down.

HOW DO YOU GET THE MOST FROM OTHERS

Delegation

There comes a point where working harder is unsustainable and working smarter by delegating is essential. Delegation is an investment. It uses time now but it saves time later. You need to free up your time to do the things that give you energy at work, so it is vital for you that you delegate and essential for more junior people to learn by doing. I would suggest that if things are not in the important row of your 'action list' then they should be delegated.

Delegation is also an art rather than a science and good delegation will be dependent on the relationship between you and the person you are delegating to as well as their knowledge and skill, but it is something you will need to be good at in order to gain promotion in your firm.

Delegation is a key skill and worthy of a book on its own but my top tips for delegation are as follows.

- Think about what the person you are delegating to is getting from doing the work — this might include new skills, exposure to other partners and staff, proof that they can do a task efficiently and effectively. Let them know what is in it for them.

- Give enough time for communicating the instructions including the wider context for the work. This saves you time in the long run.

- Check that they understand what they are being asked to do. Often requiring them to make a note of your meeting or a project plan setting out the elements that need to be considered are good methods to check their understanding.

- Agree 'check in' points to ensure you understand where they have got to and can offer appropriate help.

- Plan sufficient time for you to identify mistakes and for them to correct them; if you correct them this takes up your time and they will not learn for next time.

- Do not worry about the amount of work your juniors have. They are adults and, as long as they know that they can come to you, they will tell you when they are overloaded.

Using Those Who Have Specialist Expertise

There is very often support available within the firm you work in and if you use it effectively it can make life much easier and free up your time. I have been told by partners in many offices around the world, as well as by support staff, that they see a difference between how men and women in the firm use the support available to them. They tell me that women do not ask for help as often as men do and often try to do the support function's jobs as well as their own.

Exercise

To check that you know who is out there to help you I suggest you set out your answers to the following.

Who are the key specialist contacts in your network for:

- Business development advice and support.

- HR issues for you and your team.

- Administration support.

- The financial performance of your team.

- Marketing.

- Technical knowledge.

I suggest you populate this list and then over time meet each of these people to find out exactly what they do and how they can support you in the future.

Identifying and Using Your Support Network

We all rely on others inside and outside work. Women have a tendency to take responsibility for many tasks that others could do. Those others might include our secretaries, those we live with, cleaners and others who we work with.

Exercise
Review your network identifying those who support you at work and at home. Set out those who you rely on.

At work:

At home:

In each case:

- Is there more that you think they could do to support you?

- Have you talked to them about what more they could do to help? They may have ideas you have not thought of.

What support do you see others utilising? Could you get some of that?

It might be useful to think of this as your support network which is distinct from the development network that I talk about in Chapters 11 and 12. Chapter 11, in particular, talks more about how you can develop your network and might give you some additional ideas for developing this support network.

HOW TO GET THE MOST FROM YOUR MENTAL CAPACITY

Your firm employs you for the quality of your brain. Recent neurological advances have allowed us to understand much more about how we get the most from our brains, although it has to be said that the intricate workings of much of the brain are still not clearly understood. To explore how we can maximise the output from this sophisticated tool it is useful to understand more about how it operates. One thing to note is that your brain is a physical organ that is connected to the rest of your body. Like other organs it needs nourishment and care to operate at its maximum capacity; this has implications for how you structure your day if you want to get the best from your brain.

The components of your brain and what they do

In very simple terms and for these purposes your brain has three key operating centres (Figure 3.2):

Figure 3.2: The Tool Between Your Ears.

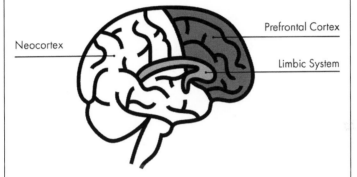

Neocortex

Prefrontal Cortex

Limbic System

The first is the limbic system. This is old in evolutionary terms and seems to hold the emotional responses to the data we take in. The limbic system is activated by external stimuli milliseconds before the other systems which means it is powerful in our decision-making processes. It has no logic and no language and its key role is not recognised by us in our logical thought.

The second is the neocortex which is the part of the brain with logic, language and conscious memories. It appears that we prefer to store mental processes in the back of the neocortex where they do not use vital energy by clogging up the prefrontal cortex.

The third sits just behind our foreheads and only consists of 5% of our brain volume. It is the prefrontal cortex which is the part of the brain we use to process new information and to think. This thin layer is a comparatively recent evolutionary development and uses significant amounts of energy.

You can experience the difference between using the neocortex and the prefrontal cortex by first asking yourself what 2×2 is. The answer comes out fast and without conscious thought. We know the answer in our neocortex as we have learned it long ago and we just need to bring it forward. In contrast, if I was to ask you what 9×123 is you would have to work it out and use your prefrontal cortex; you can feel how hard it is to get that part of your brain to work quickly and efficiently.

We will refer back to these elements and how you use them throughout this book.

HOW YOU CAN GET THE MOST FROM YOUR BRAIN IN RELATION TO TIME

When You Do Important Tasks

When we were teenagers our brains were still connecting up and there is significant evidence that they operated differently; however, some of the habits and assumptions about how our brains work stay with us from our student days. One assumption is that our brain will continue to work effectively late into the night. This is rarely true with adults. It is possible to do things easily and effectively in the morning when your brain has rested and has energy that will not be done as well later in the day when your brain function is not as good. The consequent tip is to do the important things early in the day.

It is really easy to spend the part of the day that your brain is working best on sifting through emails. This is a waste of good thinking time. My advice is to review your emails in the morning to pick out the really urgent ones and then leave the remainder until late morning so that you leave the key morning hours (10−12 a.m.) to think and work on the things that are really important to you. This is the time when you should be thinking about your career as one of the important things. Please do not be one of the women I come across that writes her annual appraisal late at night, up against the deadline because there were so many urgent (but less important) things that were done first.

Committing Vital Information to Memory

When we are asked a question that we are not prepared for, it is our limbic system that engages first and most powerfully, particularly if the person asking us the unexpected question has power over us. The logic and language of the neocortex and the analytic skills of the prefrontal cortex can desert us all (male and female alike) in these circumstances and we are left with a blank mind and the emotional desire for fight or flight, neither of which are helpful in a professional firm.

There are certain ideas that are worth thinking about and committing to your memory so that you do not need to use the prefrontal cortex under pressure. I have identified a number of these further into the book, for example, setting out clearly what you contribute to the firm and the impression you want to give to others. Preparing by giving such important matters the time, focus and attention they deserve is using your brain efficiently and ensuring that what you want to say is what comes out of your mouth. This saves you considerable time in the long run.

Assumptions and Stereotypes

In order to make the world easier to understand, and less taxing on the resources of our brains we all use the 'short-hand' of assumptions and stereotypes. This makes life easier for us as we do not need to check out all the information that is available to us. The downside is that it opens up us and others to the mis-interpretation of the facts in front of us and is the source of unconscious biases. We all use these short cuts and they will be used about you and by you. It is worth being aware that we need to test out our own assumptions of what we and others can do and to check that others are not incorrectly assuming things about us. This may take a little more time and a lot more questions and attention, but it is important to avoid misunderstandings.

My Challenges to You

1. Take your career planning seriously. It is important. Buying this book is not enough, you will also have to do some things differently.

2. Be aware of yourself and when you are working well, or not. Note the external and internal influences that

impact your well-being. Be more conscious about yourself and how you work.

3. Get organised:

- Ensure you have time booked in your diary for the things that give you energy.

- Carve out space in your diary to plan and think strategically.

- Identify and engage with those that can help you with the tasks you have.

- Use your brain for the most important tasks when it is most alert.

Tips from the top — Advice from partners to women in their firm

'Look at your diary — what is a bad habit and what is really necessary?'

'Ask for the information you need'.

'You don't have to be perfect'.

'Your career is a marathon not a sprint'.

'Get the team behind you and to support you, you need them'.

'Learn how to delegate, the team grows, the trust grows and the business grows'.

'You have to be forensic about planning your life as a partner, because your time is valuable to your family, your clients and your fellow partners'.

FURTHER RESOURCES YOU MIGHT FIND USEFUL

Rock, D. (2009) Your brain at work. *Harper Business Review*.

Schwartz, T., & McCarthy, C. (2007). Manage your energy not your time. *Harvard Business Review*, October 2007.

Covey, S. (2004, January 4). *Seven habits of highly successful people*. Simon and Schuster; Reprinted Edition.

CHAPTER 4

WHAT DO YOU OFFER YOUR FIRM?

Who am I to be brilliant, gorgeous, talented, and
fabulous? Actually, who are you not to be? You
are a child of God. Your playing small does not
serve the world.'

— Marianne Williamson, *A Return to Love*

Exercise

Before reading any further take a few moments to think
and then to set out below what it is that you offer your
firm — why are you of value to them?

●

-

-

-

-

Now review what you have written.

- Is it any different from what those who are more junior to you would be able to write?

- Is it any different from what others at your grade would be able to write?

- Does it reflect the positive feedback you have had over the years (the external view)?

- Does it show what the firm gets from you in terms of output or have you merely reflected what you put into your work?

- Does it reflect the commercial reality of what you offer the firm? What are the financial gains, for them, of employing you?

A typical response to this question that I have had in female coaching groups looks like this:

- I work really hard and for very long hours.

- Clients like me.

- I am technically good.

- I am very good at working with the juniors.

When I push harder a different picture emerges:

- I lead a team whose work is very profitable for the firm (the profit margin on my jobs this year has been $X\%$ compared with a firmwide average of $Y\%$).

- I have very strong relationship skills, which mean that clients come to me with requests for work and I am able to forge strong productive relationships at all levels within the client organisation, referring work to other parts of the firm as appropriate.

- I am creative and solution focussed in order to be able to offer the client something different. They have expressed their delight with this in their feedback on the most recent assignment. This means that they pay their bills without question, improving our working capital ratios.

- I work to develop the skills of those more junior to me in the team, so that we can push work down, maximising profit whilst maintaining quality and retaining staff. This has short-term and long-term commercial benefits for the team and the wider firm.

Exercise

Having read that how would you change what you wrote above to reflect what you actually offer the firm?

•

•

•

•

We will use this in many of the following chapters — being clear about what you offer is key to your career.

VALUING WHAT YOU BRING

It is worth noting here that we often undervalue what comes easily to us. A classic example is being good with people so that you make good relationships inside and outside the firm. This is a skill that women I work with often undervalue or simply miss out because they have not had to learn it explicitly or from a book. These are the kind of skills that will be increasingly useful to you as you rise within the firm and are very hard to develop — learn to acknowledge them and to value them.

MY CHALLENGES TO YOU

1. Write out a paragraph that reflects what you offer the firm.

2. Ensure it is senior enough and reflects what is distinctive about you.

3. Play with it and then leave it for a week before you play with it again.

4. Try it out on people you trust. Get used to saying it to other people so that you naturally start to make it a part of what you say about yourself. This practice moves it from the prefrontal cortex where you have to think about it and create it every time, to the neocortex where you can easily recall it — from conscious competence to unconscious competence.

Tips from the top — Advice from partners to women in their firm

'You need to be very clear about what you do well, and how you can make a difference. What do you bring to the business?'.

'Believe in yourself'.

'If you focus on what you are good at they will too'.

'Be prepared to be the kind of leader that you want to be and not a clone. I am different to my other partners, I discuss and don't impose. I believe in flexibility and trust. I create relationships and discussions. I see these as strengths and so do my clients'.

'Being a woman can be a great strength'.

'You have to get comfortable about talking about yourself and what you are doing'.

'You are a woman, don't pretend to be a man'.

'I was penalised for being too nice. I did some work on reframing this and now my relationship building skills are seen as my strength'.

RESOURCES

Colantuono, S. The career advice you probably didn't get. TED talk.

Saujani, R. Teach girls bravery not perfection. TED talk.

CHAPTER 5

ARE YOU AMBITIOUS? IF SO WHAT ARE YOU AMBITIOUS FOR?

*Oh, it's delightful to have ambitions. I'm so glad
I have such a lot. And there never seems to be any
end to them - that's the best of it. Just as soon as
you attain to one ambition you see another one
glittering higher up still. It does make life so
interesting.*

— L.M. Montgomery, *Anne of Green Gables*

The definition of ambition I like to use comes from
the Oxford University Press whose dictionaries
define ambition as *a strong desire to do or achieve
something.*

The purpose of this book is to help you to manage
your career actively so that you achieve your work ambitions — you get to achieve what you want to. Your
career management is not an alternative to doing excellent work with clients. It is in addition to that excellent
work. I hear many women I work with say that they do
not have the time or the energy to do more. They are

working all the hours they have. I understand this, but if you are ambitious, in that you have things you want to achieve, you do need to manage your career. However, this career management needs to be efficient, focussed and effective so that you get the maximum impact for the minimum time commitment.

My hope is that you will make the choice to manage your career actively ... because you are worth it!

WHAT ARE YOU AMBITIOUS FOR?

Let us take a step back and consider your wider ambitions for your life. Work is an important element in our lives, but it needs to live in equilibrium with, and contribute to, the other important relationships and interests in our lives. I use the word equilibrium as it does not infer strict equality nor does it infer that work is not part of our lives, which the phrase 'work/life balance' does.

Few of us have a crystal clear idea about where we want to be in the future. When I talk to women about their future aspirations they often have difficulty articulating what they want which is perfectly normal. The hopes they have exist more in the realm of the limbic part of their brain, in feelings that have not been thought through in the more rigorous neocortex with its requirement for language and logic. Many find it helpful to articulate and set out the aspirations that they do know at a rational level as it puts work ambitions into their rightful context.

WHAT DO YOU WANT YOUR LIFE TO BE LIKE IN THREE YEARS' TIME?

Planning your career does not mean you need to have an exact career path set out now; it means you are actively thinking about what you want and what you have to offer, so that when opportunities come up you are in a position to assess them and use them proactively.

Three years is long enough for things to change, but also close enough for you to imagine what life will be like. This is a chance to be honest with yourself. What do you want from your life? It may be that when you think of the life you want the first aspect you think of is work or it may be that there are other parts of your life that are your first priority. There is no right answer, only your right answer.

Exercise

What do you want to be doing in three years' time?

- How old will you be?

- How old will those who are important to you be? Name them and their ages.

    ○

    ○

    ○

- Where do you want to be living?

- What do you want to be doing in your non-work time?

- What do you want to keep unchanged from your life as it is now?

- What are the things that you would like to be different from your life as it is now?

- What further information do you need so that you are able to plan to move towards this?

- How can you get this information?

- Who do you need to get involved?

- What action do you need to take so that you are able to move towards this?

- What is the first step?

WHERE DOES YOUR WORK FIT INTO THIS LIFE?

This is very personal. My job as a coach at this point is to get you to think; to move from the limbic emotional reaction to the logic of the neocortex and the analysis of the prefrontal cortex so that you can examine what you want.

Where does work fit into in this aspirational life? Is work going to be merely a funding mechanism for this life or a key source of fulfilment in its own right?

Exercise

If it is merely a funding mechanism:

- How much money will you need to fund this life?

- What does this mean in terms of what you need to achieve at work?

- What can you do to move towards this?

- Who do you need support from to get to this?

- What is the first step?

In summary — what does this ambition mean; what do you want to achieve in your firm?

Exercise

If work will provide fulfilment in its own right:

• What do you get out of your work beyond the money?

• What do you love about your work?

• What aspects give you energy? (See Chapter 3)

• What aspects drain your energy? (See Chapter 3)

• What would your ideal job look like?

• What can you do to move towards this job?

• Who do you need support from to move into this job?

• What is the first step?

In summary — what does this ambition mean; what do you want to achieve in your firm?

I hope that from these exercises you have a clearer idea of what you want to achieve at work and who you need to support you in this, or at least what information would help you to gain clarity. These exercises are ones you might start with and then come back to, allowing your brain time to process and be creative. You might find it useful to talk through what you have written with somebody that knows you well and has no personal stake in what you want. If you have a mentor they would be very useful in such a conversation (see Chapter 12).

ARE YOU AMBITIOUS AT WORK?

In this book I have assumed that you are ambitious at work. By this I mean that part of what you want to achieve at work is promotion to the level in your firm that is commensurate with your intelligence, hard work, skills and what the firm gets from this input. This wish to get promoted to the level commensurate with what you offer the firm is not enough in itself to help you. It needs to be understood and supported by those around you.

THE COMMUNICATION MISMATCH

I have done a lot of research in professional service firms in order to design tailored women's leadership programmes for them. One of the recurring themes of this research is that the partners (male and female) say that women as a group are not as ambitious as their male peers. When I question further they say that the women do not appear as interested in promotion.

In contrast, when I ask the women within the firm if they are ambitious or interested in promotion the reply is very often an unequivocal yes. So what is going on? Why is there this mismatch?

From my experience discussing the issue with partners and women and reviewing the international research, there are a number of reasons why women are not perceived to be ambitious. At the surface level the answer comes from a number of sources.

- Women do not express their ambition as simplistically as their male peers. Women talk of 'wanting to make a difference to the organisation', to be the 'acknowledged expert' or to 'fulfil their potential'. Most men talk more simply about wanting partnership.

- Men talk about their ambition earlier, asking what they need to do to be promoted to partnership.

- Women do not use the structural opportunities available in professional service firms to focus on the future and state their ambition in the way men do. This is explored further in Chapter 17 when I look at the way men and women use their appraisals.

- Men will put themselves forward for jobs when they have as little as 60% of the requirements, whilst women will wait until they feel they have all the necessary experience and skills (Kay & Shipman, 2014).

- When approached to take a new role, women will ask questions and take time to think about it whilst men will step forward more immediately. This hesitation is perceived to indicate a lack of ambition in the women approached.

You need to be aware of these differences, but I am not asking you to behave like the men. These differences come from more complex and deeper sources and behaving like men is not the answer for you or the firm.

- There are social connotations to being an ambitious woman. Kristin van Ogtrop in her Time article notes that the phrase 'you're very ambitious' when applied to a woman is 'code for so many other things, nearly all of them bad'. This means that women are less likely to be as clear about their ambition when compared with their male peers as they are judged more harshly for overt ambition. I have come across women who were given the feedback that they failed their partnership panels because they were 'too ambitious'. I have never come across that as a reason for a male failure at their panel.

- Hardworking women in Professional Service Firms assume that they do not have to state their ambition explicitly. I have been told 'of course I am ambitious; do you think I would work those long hours if I was not?'

- At a deep societal level men are automatically assumed to be ambitious whilst women are assumed not to be and this assumption is not checked out with the individual.

YOUR CHOICE

If you are ambitious in the way I have defined it and want to progress through the grades in a professional services firm there are two alternatives:

1. You can hope that in your firm you are lucky enough to be seen and actively sponsored by partners who see your potential and take the time and trouble to find out exactly what you are doing, publicise this to other influential partners and steer your career for you. There are examples of this happening but it is a huge gamble.

2. Alternatively, you can manage your career actively.

HOW TO EXPRESS YOUR AMBITION

If you decide to manage your career actively the question of your ambition needs to be placed in the context of what you offer the firm. This is a negotiation and you need to ensure that the partner you are negotiating with understands what you are offering before you talk about what you want. This is the time to be really clear about your paragraph from the last chapter. If you have not communicated what you offer, the partner is not working with all the facts.

Expressing your ambition appears to be a really simple statement. How difficult is it to say 'I would like to get involved with this aspect of work this year' or 'I would like to be a partner in this firm in 20XX'? Actually, it is surprisingly difficult for many women (and some men). When I ask women in the coaching room to tell me what they want from the firm some leave out the date, others make the statement but then tell me all the reasons why it is not going to happen (partner' preferences, other candidates, future uncertainty etc.).

At this point, with the knowledge about the communication mismatch, I want you to look back at what you said your ambition was in your firm from the last exercise and compare it with the examples of two really clear statements:

1. 'I would like to be a partner in this firm in 20XX'.

2. 'I would like to take on X piece of work this year'.

The statements I have given above are really simple statements of fact. Like any negotiation, you are simply stating what you would like. It is not a demand and the partner that you are engaging with is at liberty to explain what you need to do to achieve what you want at that date you have given; indeed that is the partner's job.

If you do not put a date to your statement the partner is left with the view that, whilst you are interested in partnership or a particular area of work, you do not care about when it happens, which is unlikely to be the case.

If you supply all the reasons why that aspiration at that date is not possible then you are suggesting that you have thought about it and discounted it as a sensible proposition, allowing them to not think it through.

Those around you need to know what you are working towards, what you are ambitious for. If they do not know this simple truth they may make all kinds of assumptions about whether you are interested in advancement or particular assignments.

Examples of the simple truth that they need to know put clearly but in a less 'bald' way are:

> 'I am working with the aim of being a partner in this firm by 20XX. In order to achieve that I would like to have a plan that we agree which puts me in the best possible position to achieve that goal. Can we work together to formulate that plan?'

> 'I would like to get involved with the work on X this year. I can see advantages for the team and for my development in me working on X. I would like to work with you to understand what I would need to do to achieve that'.

There are a number of key points in these simple statements:

- They tell them what you want — they are not mind readers, so this is vital.

- They tell them when you want it — this is vital too; it focusses the mind and spurs both sides into action. I have seen too many people promised partnership or a particular assignment at an ill-defined point which keeps moving into the distance.

- They ask for an agreed plan — what is it that you need to do and by when, and what do they need to do and by when?

- They are not demanding partnership/the assignment nor are they asking them to promise anything. If we take partnership, they cannot promise you that there will be an accepted business case even if your personal case is brilliant. They will need to do some work and assess the situation. That is their job now they have the information from you.

- They stop without qualification. Too often we undertake both sides of the negotiation. For example 'I would like to be a partner but I realise that the numbers are not right yet and there are a number of candidates looking for the slot when the numbers do look better'. This is doing the negotiation for them. Let them tell you if your desire is feasible within the timeframe you have suggested and work with you so that you are in the best position.

WHEN TO EXPRESS YOUR AMBITION

My simple answer is now! However, not before you have planned, prepared and practiced so that your statement is received in the way that is most helpful to you.

My experience and the research suggests that men express their ambition much earlier in their careers than women. Women I have worked with have reported to me that they return from women's leadership programmes, express their ambition and get the response 'thank goodness, we are so relieved to hear that you are interested' or 'that is a surprise, we did not think you were ambitious'.

Having said that, my advice is always to plan, prepare and practice so that you can express your ambition clearly and with the awareness that the other person has not been doing the thinking that you have so you need to take them with you. You are bright, think carefully about when and where would be the most appropriate context to talk about your ambition. This may involve a number of conversations. In each case think about the other person you will be talking to. Will this be a surprise for them? What is the situation in which this statement will be most openly received? Do you have an appraisal coming up? Do you need to arrange a separate conversation? Do you need to state in arranging the meeting that this is a career conversation so that they are prepared?

Once you have decided when you are going to talk about your ambitions you need to prepare carefully. As set out in the previous chapter, think about all the things that you offer the firm and prepare a clear statement of what you want. Write these down and get somebody close to you to review what you have written so that these thoughts are readily available to the prefrontal cortex and easy to bring to mind. Then practice by saying it to others, not so that it is perfectly rehearsed, but so that when the emotions of the limbic brain are taking over you can ensure you say what you want to.

MY CHALLENGES TO YOU

Do you relate to any of the following? If so use your prefrontal cortex and its analytic qualities to challenge the veracity of what you are telling yourself. I have helped this process with my own challenges:

- I don't need to express my ambition in the way you suggest as they know I am ambitious — it is obvious. *I would challenge the truth of this. It may be obvious to you, but that does not mean that it has been spotted by the busy partners around you who may be making all kinds of assumptions about what you want. It is always worth testing out your assumptions.*

- I do not want to be seen as pushy or strident. *This is a tough one for women as statements made by women about their ambition can be seen as unattractive. Words like strident, bossy and pushy are 'female only' words. My challenge is that if you say nothing for fear of being disliked you are likely to be a popular manager whose career has stalled. You need to find a way to express your ambition that is clear, concise and factual. Plan, prepare and practice ... and then do it.*

- I am not ready yet. *This may be true, but if you do not signal that you are interested in the future others may make the assumption that you are not, particularly as many of your colleagues are actively expressing their ambition in their appraisals and other conversations.*

- I am worried they will tell me I am not ready, or that I will never make it. *If that is the case this is really useful career management information for you. You need to understand why they are saying this and what you can do to be ready. If they think you will never make it, it is important that you understand what you would need to do to change this view and what the alternatives are.*

Tips from the top — Advice from partners to women in their firm

'You need to say what you want'.

'I thought that I did not need to do anything more than a good job on the tasks that I was given; that was naïve'.

'I am in charge of my own destiny'.

'It is really important that you like what you do at work'.

'It is important to discuss your plan for partnership as a peer and show partners that you would make a brilliant fellow partner'.

'Being a partner is fun. You have authority, people listen to you, you have a peer group who support you and you can control your life'.

'You are treated differently inside and outside the firm as a partner'.

RESOURCES

Kay, K., & Shipman, C. (2014). The confidence gap. *The Atlantic Magazine*, May 2014.

van Ogtrop, K. (2015). Why ambition is not working for women. *Time Magazine*, October 12.

Shirley, S. Why do ambitious women have flat heads. TED talk.

Pink, D. Drive the surprising truth about what motivates us. RSA animation.

Anna, F. (2004). Do women lack ambition? *Harvard Business Review*.

CHAPTER 6

WHERE ARE YOU STARTING FROM? GETTING FEEDBACK

We cannot change what we are not aware of, and once we are aware, we cannot help but change.'
— Sheryl Sandberg, *Lean In: Women, Work, and the Will to Lead*

WHAT DO YOU KNOW ABOUT HOW OTHERS SEE YOU AT WORK?

Exercise
Fill this in quickly and without looking anything up

These are what they see as my strengths:	These are what they see as my weaknesses:

(*Continued*)

These are what they see as my strengths:	These are what they see as my weaknesses:

This table shows the things that you hold in your brain as the easily available picture of who you are at work. My challenge is whether this is the picture of you that others hold and if it is not, what are the implications for you and your career.

Once you have filled in this table it is worth reviewing it and answering the following questions.

- Is it balanced or can you remember more negative feedback than positive? If you can this is useful to be aware of.

- How recent is the feedback that you can remember? Often women I work with can remember negative feedback from school, but struggle to remember positive feedback from last year.

- Is it detailed enough that you know how to mitigate your weaknesses and build on your strengths?

- How closely does it follow the actual feedback that you have received in recent years? It is worth reviewing this feedback; my experience is that what we hold in our head can be a real distortion of what the actual feedback has been. This is where a development file is so useful (see Chapter 3). It allows us to check what we hold in our heads against what has actually been said most recently in feedback.

I am amazed at how many of the women I work with do not have current, meaningful feedback. This is often put down to a reluctance by those around them to provide feedback. This may be true, but there is also a personal responsibility here; why do we not insist that we are given this vital tool?

WHY IS FEEDBACK SO IMPORTANT?

Avoiding misunderstandings

If you know what others know about you there can be no misunderstandings. If you do not know what they see, you are open to delusions or self-limiting beliefs, neither of which are helpful to your career or your work.

Managing your career

Feedback is essential management information to allow you to manage yourself and others. Without it you are

doing the equivalent of sailing a ship without the naviga-
tion tools to know where you are in the ocean. You need
to know where you are so that you can utilise your
strengths and mitigate your weaknesses, the equivalent of
navigating towards where you want to be.

Understanding your strengths

Feedback on your strengths allows you to really understand them. This is important for your confidence and for
your work. I find that women often dismiss their
strengths; just because you find something easy it does
not mean that it is easy for others. Be aware of what
others see as your strengths.

Understanding your weaknesses

Feedback on your weaknesses allows you to address
them or avoid situations where they will be an issue. It is
very valuable to have real examples so that you understand when and where others see the weaknesses.
Feedback allows you to focus on what is important,
spending your precious development time productively.

Promotions

If you are looking for progression at work you need to
know how you are viewed against the firm's requirements; it is this view that will be used to assess you. You
need to know what the perceptions are so that you can
challenge them if they are wrong. If you understand your

perceived weaknesses then you can understand where the gaps are between where you are perceived to be and what is required for promotion. This may require you to work on the perceptions or on the reality of what you do; in either case there is work to do.

WHAT KIND OF FEEDBACK DO YOU NEED?

Think about what you are trying to achieve. Do you want to know how you are viewed generally in the partnership in order to manage your career? Do you need to know how important decision makers view you in order to prepare for a promotion? Are there specific points that you are working on and would it be useful to know how you are seen to be doing in these areas?

Feedback comes in two forms: anonymous and attributable. Anonymous feedback is incredibly useful to see the general impression we give. Those around you are more likely to be honest, but without specific examples the feedback is less useful. I often liken it to a landscape painting by an impressionist artist as it shows the general terrain but not any of the detail. A comment such as 'you lack impact' is interesting but not as useful as 'when you attend client meetings you are quiet'.

This is where attributable feedback has power; it fills in the detail by giving you specifics and allowing you to understand more. By letting you know that it is specifically in the client meetings that you are seen to be quiet and less impactful, you have the chance to understand what is going on and address the issues.

A SIMPLE MODEL FOR ATTRIBUTABLE FEEDBACK

The key things here are to get balanced feedback, with examples. The model I have found that works effectively in professional service firms is asking for feedback in the following way:

I am working on my own development and to ensure I am fully aware of my strengths and the areas I need to develop I would be grateful if you would help me by giving me:

- *3 things that I do well with examples*

- *3 things that I could do differently with examples.*

The wording is important. By asking for things that you 'could do differently', junior staff who would be reluctant to talk about your weaknesses are more likely to give you a balanced feedback. The request for three of each category pushes them to consider a more balanced view and is more likely to elicit useful feedback as to your weaknesses as well as offering useful advice as to what you could do differently.

IS ALL FEEDBACK EQUALLY IMPORTANT?

The answer to this is no. Things that make the feedback more useful are:

- If it is part of a pattern. We will all get feedback that says more about the giver than it does about us, but if there is a pattern so that you are getting similar feedback from a number of sources, then it is more use-ful and you need to consider it more carefully.

- The more specific the feedback is the more weight and importance should be attached to it.

- Client feedback is given the most weight by those inside the firm followed in importance by partner feedback.

- Written feedback is more useful than verbal.

- The source of the feedback — if the feedback is given by somebody who has power over your career it is more important and you need to understand it fully.

SPECIFIC FEEDBACK

If you are working on developing knowledge or a particu-lar skill, one way to measure how you are getting on is to ask for specific feedback. If I have been told that I lack impact in client meetings and am working on making more of an impact by speaking more, it would be useful to know how I am doing in those meetings.

The key here is to identify somebody you trust to be hon-est and to alert them that you will be asking them for feed-back so that they are prepared and collecting data. In my example I might ask somebody in the meeting to pay partic-ular attention to how I operate in the meeting so that they can give me feedback on the impact my changes are making.

WHEN SHOULD YOU ASK FOR FEEDBACK?

Feedback is best when the situation that it relates to is fresh in the giver's mind (and in yours), so my advice is to ask for feedback regularly. If you need prompts ask for it at the end of projects or every 3 months, whichever is the shorter. You might want to put these prompts in your diary.

WHERE SHOULD YOU KEEP YOUR FEEDBACK?

Please keep your feedback in a place that you can find it. You will need it for appraisals and promotion processes. Please do not be the coachee who knows she has brilliant feedback from a key client about her commercial awareness but cannot find it among all her Emails!

My tip would be to keep your feedback in your development file (see Chapter 3).

MY CHALLENGES TO YOU

Over the years I have heard a lot of reasons why people have not asked for feedback. Few bear closer examination. Here are a few for you to consider. Do you relate to any of these statements? If so stop and use the analytical skills of your prefrontal cortex to examine the veracity of what you are telling yourself. I have stated the challenges below:

I don't want to bother busy people. *BUT in professional service firms we sell the skills of our people so it is essential to these busy people that you are as clear as possible about your strengths and weaknesses; indeed it is a commercial necessity and in their interests.*

I already know what they think. *BUT this is rarely true if we have not asked them. We carry around views of ourselves from earlier on in our lives and if we do not get objective validation or challenge to those views we are unlikely to be right about what others really think of our skills.*

My career is not important enough to step forward and bother them *BUT if it is not important enough to you to step forward then it will certainly not be important to anybody else.*

I don't want to know the negative bits of the feedback I might get. *BUT it is rare that the negative shocks will be more intense than the positive surprises. My experience has been that we imagine the worst and are surprised by how positive others are. Even a nasty surprise now is better than wasting a lot of time blindly going in the wrong direction.*

Tips from the top — Advice from partners to women in their firm

'If clients are saying how good you are take advantage of this'.

RESOURCE

Correll, S., & Simard, C. (2016). Vague feedback is holding women back. *Harvard Business Review*, April 29, 2016.

CHAPTER 7

TAKING STOCK

Who in the world am I? Ah, that's the great puzzle!

— Lewis Carroll, *Alice's Adventures in Wonderland*

Exercise

The questions on the next pages are designed to help you construct a summary of your Strengths/Weaknesses/Opportunities/Threats (SWOT) at this stage in your career so that you can review and strategically analyse where you are and where you might go next. In professional service firms we do this exercise for clients and potential clients to think strategically about their place in the market. You are as important as these clients and you need to think strategically about your place in the firm.

My strengths	My opportunities
My weaknesses/development areas	The threats to what I want to achieve

MY STRENGTHS

Use the following questions to fill in the SWOT analysis strengths box.

- What is your assessment of your strengths?
  - What are you passionate about doing?
  - What are you really good at?
  - Under what circumstances do you flourish?
  - What are you something of an authority on?
  - What comes naturally and easily to you?
- What do others say are your strengths?
  - What do others come to you for?
  - What would others at work say your strengths are? *Review your appraisals and client feedback to ensure you really understand what others have said.*
  - What have others outside work identified as your strengths?
- What have been your major achievements?
- What is unique about your particular combination of skills, knowledge, experience and abilities? Think about:
  - Your technical expertise
  - Your commercial experience
  - Your experience outside the firm
  - Your international experience

- How strong are your:
  - client relationship skills?
  - financial/business management skills?

WEAKNESSES/DEVELOPMENT AREAS

Use the following questions to fill in the SWOT analysis weaknesses box.

- What is your assessment of your weaknesses?
  - What are your weaknesses?
  - What do you avoid?
  - What have you had the most difficulty with?
- What do others say?
  - What have others at work observed as your weaknesses? *Review your appraisals and client feedback to ensure you really understand what others have said.*
  - What have others outside work observed as your weaknesses?
- Under what circumstances do you not bring out your best?
- What has not gone the way you wanted it to at work?
  - What was your part in this?
- What areas would you like to develop?

OPPORTUNITIES

Use the following questions to fill in the SWOT analysis opportunities box:

- What opportunities are there to use your strengths at work?
- What opportunities are there to address your weaknesses?
  - What are the exciting, interesting new factors in your environment?
  - What are the possibilities that flow from recent changes?
- Who could help?
  - Identify who might support you.
  - Have you got a mentor?
  - Who can help you generate ideas and plans?
  - Who else needs to be in your network to support you?
  - In particular, which partners can help you?
  - Who else do you need to talk to?
- Looking internally
  - What are the opportunities available to you from the firm's learning and development function or external programmes?
  - Where can you contribute to the business? Think about:
    - Knowledge and learning

- Recruitment

- Corporate social responsibility

- Firm-wide projects, etc.

- Looking externally:

  - What client opportunities are there?

  - What are the gaps in the market?

- How can you find out about more opportunities?

THREATS

Use the following questions to fill in the SWOT analysis threats section.

- External

  - Do the people who have power over your career know of your career ambitions?

  - What are the external threats or challenges to you having the career or business you want?

  - What are the problems, barriers or difficulties in your working environment?

- Internal

  - What is stopping you from giving your best?

    - What is your part in this?

    - What part do others play in this?

- What are the things that you do that threaten you having the career or business you want?

REVIEW YOUR SWOT ANALYSIS

Given this assessment of your strengths and weaknesses, what are you going to do to exploit the opportunities you are aware of?

What support do you need?

What is your first step?

Given this assessment of your strengths and weaknesses, what are you going to do to mitigate the threats you are aware of?

What support do you need?

What is your first step?

MY CHALLENGES TO YOU

1. Sit down and actually do the SWOT. It is easy to think you know what would go in the boxes; it is only by actually doing it that you get the learning — you are important, use that powerful brain of yours to analyse where you are.

2. Once you have had a first go at the SWOT, review it in the light of what you have analysed in the last few chapters; what you offer the firm, your ambitions and the feedback you have been given.

3. Once you have done the SWOT analysis and reviewed in the context of other information available to you, show it to somebody you trust and who knows what you do. Ask them to review it for you.

RESOURCE

Mohr, T. Playing big. TED talk.

CHAPTER 8

IMPRESSION MANAGEMENT — WHAT DO YOU DO AND HOW DO YOU TALK ABOUT IT?

There is strong evidence that our work ratings, bonuses, and promotions are weakly correlated to actual performance — in fact, performance may even matter less to our success than our political skills and how we are perceived by those who make the decisions
— Michael C. Wenderoth, *Harvard Business Review*, July 2016

WHAT IS YOUR POSITION — PEACOCK, MOUSE OR ...?

Do you believe that you have a binary choice between:

1. Taking the spotlight whenever you can to talk to everybody about what you have done and the fabulous impact it has had; and

2. Working really hard with your team so that your
   work speaks for you.

This binary choice could be described as the choice
between the peacock and the mouse. One strutting
around showing their wares and the other working away
in a corner.

Many women I have worked with talk about this
choice and do see it as binary. They have come through a
school system where good work is rewarded by a teacher
taking the time to mark their essay and they see those
that take the additional step of talking about their
achievements as 'blowing their own trumpet', 'bragging',
'all mouth and no trousers' and 'playing politics'. Each of
these pejorative descriptions are accompanied with a nose
wrinkle as if the very idea elicits a bad smell, particularly
if the person doing it is a woman. When the choice is the
peacock or the mouse, with all the opprobrium heaped
on a woman trying to be a peacock, they choose mouse
and hope others will take the time to look into their corner and see what they have done.

The choice is not binary, there is a third position that
women often overlook; it is the position where you simply tell other people what you do and the impact of your
work. There is no exaggeration in this position, it is simply passing information to others who are busy and do
not have the time to come and look at what you are
doing. These others need information to make informed
decisions about you and you are not helping yourself, or
them, by simply working hard and expecting them to
make all the effort to understand your achievements. I
am not sure there is an animal analogy that I can use for

this third position — perhaps it is simply the adult human position.

Why managing your impression is not 'blowing your own trumpet' and is helpful to partners

- They are busy people.

- They need to know about you so that they can make decisions about your career in an informed way.

- They are bombarded with data and need information to make their decisions, but this information needs to be clear and easy to find.

WHAT IS IMPRESSION MANAGEMENT?

The best definition I have found is that it is managing the perceptions others have of you. Other definitions that I have heard used are:

- Managing what others say about you when you are not there

- Communicating your unique selling proposition (USP)

- Communicating your personal brand

This is not the black art of manipulation, nor is it pretending you are something that you are not. It is not a replacement for excellent work. This is simply ensuring that other people know the truth, and particularly the current truth, about you and what you do. It is ensuring that they are not working on impressions, half-truths or old truths.

If you have been with the firm for a number of years it is likely that there are partners who came across you as a graduate trainee or junior and have not seen you since. Their impression of you is old and out of date, but they do not know that.

WHY IS IMPRESSION MANAGEMENT IMPORTANT?

Impression management is not a substitute for excellent work, but it is a necessary accompaniment.

To put it at its most brutal:

- Unless your brilliant work is known about and talked about when you are not there, this brilliant work is worthless for your career.

- If your brilliant work is known about you are likely to get more interesting work.

- If your brilliant work is known about you will be considered for promotions, pay raises and bonuses.

- If your brilliant work is known about you are more likely to achieve what you want to achieve at work.

It would be lovely if professional service firms worked on the basis that senior people had enough time to investigate what those working for them have done; sadly, with the pressure on time, this is not what happens. Partners rely on those who work for them to do excellent work *and* to communicate this to them in a way that is easy to assimilate and remember.

WHAT DO YOU WANT THEM TO BE SAYING ABOUT YOU WHEN YOU ARE NOT THERE?

Exercise
Write down three things that you would like people to say about you

1.

2.

3.

Now step outside yourself and have a really good look at those three things that you have written down. Are they really what you want partners to be saying about you? Do they differentiate you from others? Could they be said about more junior colleagues? Do they tie in with what you wrote in the final exercise of Chapter 4 when you set out what you offer the firm?

If you have written 'hard-working' — is this not a prerequisite for working in your firm?

If you have written 'a safe pair of hands' does that really reflect what you do?

If you have written 'good at training the juniors' think carefully. This is a key task in any team, but you are expressing it in a way that can be under valued. An alternative might be 'improving the profitability of the group by ensuring the juniors can take on more complex work'.

Think about the partners around you and other role models. What are they known for? How does your USP complement or blend in with theirs?

Think about the feedback you have had in Chapter 6. What are they already saying about you and how would you want to build on that to reflect the current reality?

Try to be clear and concise. If you are not clear about what you are offering, it is hard for others to be.

Exercise
Have another go — what do you really want people to say about you?

1.

2.

3.

YOUR CHOICE

Now that you have decided what you want them to say about you, you have a choice. You can:

1. Leave it to chance:

   ○ Trust that the systems in your firm are fair and uti-lise all the current information available.

   ○ Trust that the partners are omniscient.

   ○ Trust that the partners are taking the time to under-stand what you are doing.

2. Manage the impression others have of you so that it reflects the truth:

   ○ No lying or exaggeration

   ○ Ensuring they know the current truth

My experience is that even in the most fabulous firms the conditions for leaving it to chance do not exist and you need to get involved.

HOW DO YOU MANAGE THE PERCEPTION OTHERS HAVE OF YOU?

Assuming that you decide to manage your brand rather than leaving it to chance, how do you do this? You have already done much of the hard work.

1. You have already done the first step, which is being clear about what you offer the firm. You did this in Chapter 4.

2. The second step has also been done — being clear about what others' perceptions of you are by looking at the feedback in Chapter 6. This is useful information to help you craft your message, ensuring any misapprehensions or incorrect assumptions are challenged.

3. The third step is deciding the three clear messages about you which you have identified in the last challenge.

4. The final step is to talk to others about what you are currently doing.

HOW TO TALK ABOUT WHAT YOU ARE DOING

There are many opportunities to talk about and communicate what you are doing for the firm. Partners are the owners of the firm and are genuinely interested; what you are doing has commercial and reputational implications for them.

Use the three things you crafted above as a base and now describe what you are doing at work. Ideally find a piece of work that you are doing that you feel passionate about and shows off what you offer the firm.

My suggestion is that you take the work you are currently doing and draft a short paragraph that shows you at your BEST. It needs to be:

- Brief — people's attention span is short

- Enthusiastic — show off what you love doing. Enthusiasm is infectious and they will feel it

- Successful — show what you are contributing to the firm

- Take-aways — make the links between yourself and the successful work you are doing so that they will remember the link when they next think about you

An answer to the question 'how are things going for you?' might be 'Things are good. I am currently working on X which is fascinating. It is a new area for the firm and I think this work should open up a really lucrative market for us. The client was delighted and with their feedback I think we should get more work from them and other clients with the same issues. How are you?'

Exercise
How would you describe your current situation so that you are showing your BEST?

Review This Against the BEST Criteria

This example and the consequent description will need changing, perhaps every quarter, but as new work comes in think about how you want to talk about it. This is a skill that will become natural as you practice it.

Be clear about what is in it for the firm. Is there big money involved, an expanding market, cross selling opportunities or a reputational issue? Be prepared to use numbers to show the size of what you are working on — they catch people's attention.

If you are leading something say 'I am leading the team that …'. Avoid the phrases 'working for' unless that is your only role. People will be interested in what you are doing; avoid those words that undermine your message such as 'just', 'quite' and 'a bit'.

This does need to be crafted and prepared. It is very unlikely that you will come out with what you want to say without preparation and practice. As set out in Chapter 3, analysis before you are in the situation will allow your brain to work most effectively.

When we are chatting by the coffee machine or in the general small talk at the start or end of meetings, there are some standard replies that communicate unstated but important messages which you need to be aware of.

For example, in response to the greeting 'how are you?' many of us respond:

- 'I am fine' — the subtext here is that 'I really don't have the time or interest to tell you more'.

- 'I am busy' — here the subtext is 'I really could not take on any more work no matter how fascinating it is'.

- I am 'stressed' — the subtext is that you are really not managing the work you are already doing and this may put people off giving you their work.

Here I am exaggerating for effect but I think you will see my point.

WHO TO TALK TO ABOUT WHAT YOU
ARE DOING

The partners you work for are busy and will appreciate help in understanding what you are doing so that they have a more rounded picture beyond the specifics of the project you are working with them on. You might want to talk to them and agree how they would like to get information about what you are doing to ensure that they are getting information in a form that they find most useful.

Many I have worked with send their partner a short factual email every month setting out the things that they are doing and have accomplished. In particular, it is essential that your sponsor (see Chapter 12) and your supporters in the firm know what you are up to. They will be talking about you when you are not there and they need to know this factual information, a written note gives them information that they can refer to when needed. If you decide to send a monthly factual update, I suggest you put a reminder in your diary to prompt you and set up a draft email at the start of the month that you update as you go along to record the things that you want to say. This makes it easy for you and is helpful for the partners to know for planning work, making informed decisions about you and communicating with others — it is not 'blowing your own trumpet'.

If you have feedback from clients ensure that the appropriate people for your work and your career see this. You might want to include it in your monthly update or simply pass in on to the partners who have an interest in the client or in you and mention it in the update. This is information that they need to know about.

WHAT OTHER INFORMATION IS OUT THERE ABOUT YOU

The information about you that people can access without you is most powerful for you if it is current and consistent in its underlying messages.

It is worth looking up all your biographies that are sitting on your firm's systems. Often there are more than one (HR, Marketing and other departments may have their own old versions) and some of them can be really unhelpful. Just because you do not use the old ones does not mean that partners will not access them when they are looking you up and considering you in your absence for client jobs or promotions.

Ensure that your biographies internally, on the firm's web site and on LinkedIn (and other similar systems) are consistent and show off the clear messages that you want to be communicated about you. Many firms have guidance on what you should have on LinkedIn and similar professional networks. Have you looked at this? Have you looked at what your peers, the partners around you and your competitors in other firms have publically available — there is much you could learn from these (good and bad) and your clients will be accessing this information.

Lastly look at the pictures that accompany your biographies. Were they taken when you first joined the firm? Do they show you on holiday or in a social situation? Ensure that you have a picture that is professional, shows the woman you are now and is consistent with the messages about yourself that you want others to have.

MY CHALLENGES TO YOU

What others think about you will be taken partly from the quality of your work and also from what you say and they read about you. This needs your conscious management, do not leave it to chance.

1. Make time for thinking and working on this when your brain is at its best. It will not take long, but it does need your focus and care. Perhaps you could consider it as part of your meeting with MS (see Chapter 3).

2. Use your diary to prompt you to send updates.

3. Manage the assumptions that are made about you — others are busy and simple assumptions are easy but not necessarily correct. You have a responsibility to help others see the current truth.

4. Be very clear about what you want others to say about you and ensure that you are consistently reinforcing these messages and passing them on to those around you.

Tips from the top — Advice from partners to women in their firm

'Remember you have a network. Tell them what you do and what you want. Start with the basics, what you are passionate about and don't assume people know what you do'.

'Don't underestimate the importance of an elevator pitch — it is vital'.

'Perception is even more important than performance which is hard to hear'.

'I know myself and have no problems talking about my strengths and my weaknesses'.

RESOURCES

Wenderoth, M. C. (2016). Great leaders embrace office politics. *Harvard Business Review*, July.

Ibarra, H. (2015). *Act like a leader think like a leader*. Boston, MA, Harvard Business Review Press.

Mohr, T. Playing big. TED talk.

CHAPTER 9

POLITICS — HOW DO YOU GET INVOLVED?

The only thing necessary for the triumph of evil is for good men to do nothing.

— Edmund Burke

Is your firm a pure meritocracy or a political bear pit? The truth is that it is likely to be both. To survive and thrive in any professional service firm you need to be excellent at work <u>and</u> be able to navigate the politics. It is perfectly possible to do this with grace and integrity, but to do so you need to understand what is going on. It is not possible to avoid politics in any professional service firm.

My experience is that professional service firms are extremely political organisations. Every partner is an owner and rightly sees the firm as theirs; however, there is a management system laid over this disparate owner-ship which is designed to pull the whole partnership in one unified direction. Partners have told me that leadership in these situations is like herding cats, albeit extraordinarily bright, entrepreneurial cats.

The women I work with often have a visceral reaction to the politics at play in their firm. I have heard comments like 'I do not play politics', 'it makes me squirm to see others play politics', and 'I do not have time for these games, I am getting on with my work'.

For those of you that recognise these statements, let me re-frame what we mean by politics. The dictionary definition of politics that I like is *social relations involving authority or power*. By this definition the politics going on in your firm is entirely value neutral; it is not good or bad, it simply is the way people interact in situations outside the family (and often inside families too). It is why politics exists in the school yard and in every club and working situation you will ever encounter. Politics just exists when people get together. It is a fact of life.

It is how you play the politics that is the choice.

You can decide not to get involved. This is a perfectly legitimate choice but the consequence is a bit like a player sitting in the middle of a football pitch with their hands over their ears and their eyes closed. They are now an obstruction to those around them and absolutely no use to themselves.

You can decide to get involved, but how you do so then becomes a further choice. A number of wonderful colleagues I worked with at Cranfield University have provided the structure and interpretation that women I have worked with found extremely helpful. Kim Turnbull-James (with Tanya Arroba and Simon Baddeley) created the most useful political map I have

come across (Baddeley & James, 1987) and our colleague
Sandy Cotter further developed this in her teaching.
Initially the map reflects what many women I work with
think about politics. It shows a one-dimensional line, as
illustrated in **Figure 9.1**, showing a continuum between
those with a self-focus and those with an organisational
focus (but taking the self into account). This correlates
with what many believe: people who care only about
themselves and their advancement are the ones who get
involved in politics in the organisation — politics is done
at the left-hand side of this continuum. They believe that
those who care more about the organisation do not play
politics.

Figure 9.1: Who "Plays Politics" a One Dimensional View.

ORIENTATION

SELF ◄─────────────────────────► **ORGANISATION**

EGO DRIVEN   GUIDED BY CONCERNS BEYOND MY
                                              OWN EGO

Play politics   **Are above politics**

However, Kim rightly shows that this one dimension
is not enough to show what goes on in organisational
life. She adds a vertical line showing the ability and willingness to read the situation. That is, the ability and
willingness to see what the real agendas are, where the
real power lies and where the alliances are. For example, in partnerships the real power is often not with the
person who has the title but the person who held the
title before; the eminence grise who has returned to client work, but wields the most influential voice in any
partners meeting.

Figure 9.2: How You Engage with Politics.

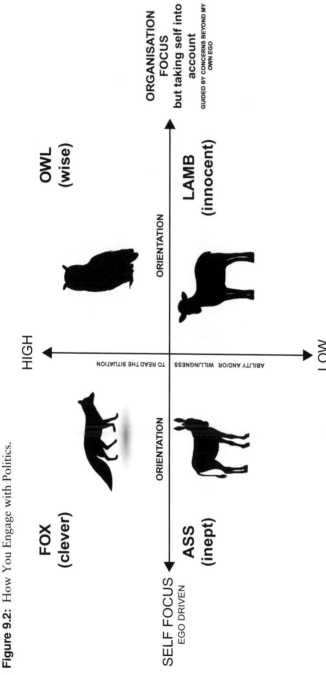

FOX
(clever)

OWL
(wise)

ASS
(inept)

LAMB
(innocent)

HIGH

LOW

ABILITY AND/OR WILLINGNESS   TO READ THE SITUATION

ORIENTATION

ORIENTATION

SELF FOCUS
EGO DRIVEN

ORGANISATION
FOCUS
but taking self into
account
GUIDED BY CONCERNS BEYOND MY
OWN EGO

As you can see from **Figure 9.2**, there are four characters who inhabit this political map and my experience is that these are archetypes that work in different cultures internationally. None of us inhabits only one quartile of this political map; we can move and display different attributes at different times, but the map gives us a useful vocabulary to indicate our own behaviour and that of those around us.

THE CLEVER FOXES

This behaviour gets rewards in a professional service firm. Behaving like a fox is clever, they have a real understanding as to what is going on and you can learn a lot from those who act like foxes. They are out for themselves, but they know how to position themselves and others to gain advantage. They make good mentors and sponsors, but you need to be aware that they are playing the politics for their own good and if and when your agenda diverges from theirs they will not support you and will sacrifice you to ensure their own needs are met.

THE INEPT ASSES

Culturally these are sometimes also 'the bull (or elephant) in a china shop'. Those that habitually behave in this way do not last long in the cut-throat environment of a professional service firm. Their self-centred view is easy to spot and they self-destruct without the situational awareness to cover their tracks. They are hard to handle if you are

their manager, but they are unlikely to cause you any
long-term problems in progressing your career.

THE INNOCENT LAMBS

If you have ever come away from an important meeting
feeling frustrated because a decision was made that was
illogical or badly thought through, there may well have
been others involved in the meeting that were more politically aware. Without your knowledge they may have
been involved in pre-meetings with the key influencers to
canvas for their position, meaning that the logical argu-
ments used in the meeting were already doomed to failure. They were acting with situational awareness and you
were the innocent lamb.

Lambs are naïve and if you think that by ignoring the
politics around you, you are doing the best for yourself,
your team and your firm, I would suggest that this may
be where your behaviour is putting you on this political
map. Lambs are lovely, but there are three outcomes to
behaving like a lamb:

- You follow the flock and look like all other lambs

- You are fleeced

- You are slaughtered

Put simply, this is a dangerous position. Alliances are being
made around you, but lambs' unwillingness or inability to
see where the real power is and what the real agenda consists
of leaves them open to unexpected and unpleasant surprises.

THE WISE OWLS

It is possible to act with total integrity and be wise to the politics. The archetype of the wise owl embodies the ability to look after oneself, one's team and the wider community. Owls take a broad and 360-degree view of what is going on and can see in the day and the night. Like the fox they kill, but unlike the fox who kill for fun they do this only to feed themselves and their brood.

In this model the wise owl in the firm is aware of the alliances around her, she understands what those with influence and power are seeking to achieve and the wider context. She uses that knowledge to support her team, her firm and her own career.

HOW TO USE THIS MAP

The first use is to look at your network.

- Who do you know that displays the behaviour of the wise owl — they make brilliant sponsors and mentors. Think about how you can engage with and learn from them.

- Where are your colleagues that behave like sly foxes? Do not dismiss them as bad, they also make fabulous sponsors and mentors, but with one proviso. When in 'fox mode' they will abandon you as soon as your agenda gets in the way of theirs. Think about how you can engage with and learn from them without being harmed by them.

The second is to understand the rules of the political game. These include:

- **Produce excellent work**. Your professional service firm is likely to pride itself on being a meritocracy and the production of excellent work is a fundamental requirement to your survival and progression in the firm. A stellar performance is necessary, but not sufficient, for you to advance.

- **Disclosure.** Just think about what you tell others at work. I would never advocate saying anything other than the truth, but you do not need to reveal all of the truth all of the time to all of those around you. For example, if you are daunted by speaking in public you do not need to tell everybody. Disclose it appropriately to ensure you get the support you need to ensure it is something you can do with less fear.

- **Framing.** Just think about how you talk about what you do. 'I don't have much impact in large meetings' leaves people with an impression of you that may be neither advantageous to your career, nor indeed the whole truth. An alternative is, 'I have had the feedback that I can lack impact in large meetings and have been working on this through training courses. The feedback has been that I am much more impactful, but there is always still work to do'. As long as this is true, it gives the impression of somebody who knows their weaknesses and is proactive about working on them.

- **Alliances.** Who also wants the decision to go the way you want? Do they know what you are proposing? What is the advantage of what you want for others around you? Do they realise what is in it for them? Making alliances, by making others aware of the advantages for them sounds as if you are being Machiavellian, but it is simply being clear about the advantages of what you are proposing. This is why the conversations before meetings happen. If you believe in what you are proposing, you need to make allies by talking to others about the advantages of your proposition before important meetings, if for no other reason than people need time to think. It is also likely that others with differing agendas will be giving the facts from their perspective and you need to ensure that what you propose gets equal exposure before the meeting.

MY CHALLENGES TO YOU

1. Draw out your network. Who are the owls in your team? Who are the foxes? Who are the lambs? Who are the asses? What can you learn from them? How do you engage with them to get the output you need?

2. When you are preparing for an important meeting think about the alliances you need to make. Don't just prepare the factual content of the meeting; think about who you need to influence, and when and how you are going to do this?

Tips from the top — Advice from partners to women in their firm

'Always keep an eye on the political environment at all levels'.

'Understand the politics and who has influence in the firm'.

'Always think about the audience you are talking to'.

'You don't have to be liked by everybody and if you try you will exhaust yourself'.

RESOURCES

Baddeley, S., & James, K. T. (1987). Owl, fox, donkey or sheep: Political skills for managers. *Management Education and Development.*

Tannen, D. (2013). The power of talk: Who gets heard and why. *HBR's 10 Must Reads on Communication.*

Wenderoth, M. C. (2016). Great leaders embrace office politics. *Harvard Business Review*, July.

CHAPTER 10

STEPPING FORWARD

Action expresses priorities.
— Mahatma Gandhi

Exercise

Rate yourself using a scale between never and always as to how often you step forward and volunteer for key assignments and high-profile roles. Compare this with a peer and a person more senior than you each of whom are perceived to be high fliers.

How often do you step forward and volunteer for key roles and assignments

You

A peer

Never   Always

Somebody successful above you

If you are stepping forward as often as high fliers around you then this chapter may not be useful to you and you might want to skip it, but I would urge you to at least skim read it as the perception is that women do not step forward in the way men do.

When I interview partners in professional service firms about the differences they see between the men and the women in their firms, they often talk about how reluctant women at all levels are to step forward and volunteer for key assignments and roles. They also remark on the fact that when offered such prestigious positions women hesitate and do not appear keen. Some partners have told me with open incredulity that they have had to actively persuade women to take on prestigious and remunerative roles. In some cases this behaviour is attributed to women's childcare responsibilities, in others their lack of confidence or thirdly a lack of ambition.

Having worked with over a thousand women from professional service firms, whilst I recognise the reluctance these partners identify, I am not convinced by any of these explanations. It appears to me that assumptions are being made about women's reasoning. Not all women have children and those that do are not always the primary carer; further, the women I have worked with are very confident in their skills and abilities. I hope I have already covered the fallacy of women's lack of ambition in Chapter 5.

I think there are a number of interlocking hurdles that men do not experience but woman have to navigate before they step forward. I have set out my top six below; some may not apply to you, but it is worth thinking carefully about whether they do before we examine the important question 'so what?'.

HURDLES THAT WOMEN HAVE TO NAVIGATE THEIR WAY AROUND BEFORE STEPPING FORWARD

1. How society views women who step forward

Sheryl Sandberg talked about the first hurdle in her book *Lean in* "*Success and likeability are positively correlated for men and negatively for women. When a man is successful, he is liked by both men and women. When a woman is successful, people of both genders like her less*". What this results in is a social cost for women in taking a step forward. A number of the women I have worked with expressed concerns about taking leadership roles that mean that they are no longer 'one of the team'.

2. A reliance on 'the system'

Many of the women that I work with are very reliant on the logic of their firm's formal career system. They believe that the firm's systems will result in a meritocracy and that their good work will be recognised. Using this belief system they do not need to step forward and explicitly alert others to their interest in advancement or particular roles.

3. Getting caught in the role of doing the 'organisational dusting'

Organisational dusting is work that is not apparent if it is done well and is thus easily overlooked, but it is

clear when this work is not done well and the equivalent of 'organisational detritus' is apparent for all to
see. Organisational dusting is a role that I see women
both stepping forward for and being given. Such roles
are vital to the organisational health of the firm, but
women themselves and those who give them the 'dusting' roles, do not position this work for its commercial
contribution. An example of this is engaging and
developing the junior associates. This is a vital role
that will allow the firm to maximise profits by pushing
work down and minimise costs by aiding retention,
but is often not explicitly valued and very often done
by women. To see this operating in your firm ask
yourself how many of those fee-earners with HR
responsibilities in your firm are women and how is
that role valued internally when compared with those
that have more explicitly commercial responsibilities?

An example given to me by a partner is that
women can be more conscientious and organised (see
below for the reasons that this might be the case).
They therefore often get asked to do the organisational
aspects of projects and client liaison or naturally take
on those roles. The example given was of a female
junior who did all the work to get an important client
meeting set-up. This involved aspects of influence, client relationship building and organisational skills. In
the meeting she took the notes, whilst her male peer
was able to concentrate on the flow of the dialogue
and his contribution. The result was that he was able
to speak up with a vital point — consequently he will
be remembered by the key partners and clients at the
meeting and she will not.

4. A fear of failure. Including how women internalise failure

The driving force that has propelled successful women to the academic and career successes required for their positions in professional service firms is often a fear of failure. The resulting drive for perfection is powerful and wonderful in their early careers when achievement is more binary, but can be a hurdle later in their careers when it stops them from stepping forward for fear of being judged and failing. Many women are very hard on themselves and are more likely to see any failure as a result of their deficiencies, for example, believing 'I will be seen as inadequate if I do not take on all the work I am given'. Men are more likely to see the role others have in failure — 'it is unrealistic of my partner to think that I can take on more or work any harder'.

The paranoia that is so useful early on in women's careers (creating the momentum to achieve in all areas of their lives) can tip over and result in a lack of confidence. Women second guess themselves. They need to learn that it is OK to fail and perfection is not possible. One female partner noted that her learning point was that the key thing is not to fail at the same thing two days in a row. The fear of failure can result in inertia and perceived passivity which is interpreted as a disinterest in advancement.

This search for being perfect is not only an issue for the women in professional service firms, but research shows that it is far more prevalent in women and it has implications for the way women behave in terms of putting themselves forward for activities and entering promotion processes.

5. The attribution of success. Externalising the causes of achievement

Both anecdotal stories and research suggest that women are more likely to externalise the reasons for their success, attributing it to a great team, luck or an easy assignment. In contrast women internalise the reasons for their task's failures suggesting that they personally did not do what was needed. Men are more likely to reverse this and externalise the reasons for their failure, blaming unrealistic time frames, poor team make up and bad luck. In contrast, men tend to internalise the reasons for success, citing good leadership and clear focus. Neither extreme can be true and neither is helpful, but if the story women are telling themselves inappropriately allocates the blame or glory then it is not conducive to stepping forward.

6. A need to prepare

This search for perfection and a tendency to self-blame come with a side effect — the need to be fully prepared for every step. This is helpful in client engagements but is often overplayed in relation to the woman taking on new and challenging assignments. The resultant hesitation in stepping forward is seen by those around them as a lack of confidence in their ability or a lack of interest in the role or assignment. I think this is a fundamental misunderstanding. Women appear to need more time and space to think through the implications of a step forward. This is why women's leadership programmes get such great reviews, apart from the excellent content, they can act as that safe space to draw back and reflect, allowing participants to gather their resources in order to step forward.

SO WHAT?

To get the recognition you deserve and the career you want you will need to step up and step forward at certain key points.

1. **Work smarter not harder**

Your firm is not a pure meritocracy; if what got you here is hard work and a focus on the task, you need to be aware that this is necessary but not sufficient to move forward. Getting what you want does not necessarily involve more work; in most cases it involves being wise — employing the reflective wisdom of the owl rather than the naïve nervousness of the lamb. The political map and rules from Chapter 9 are vital here.

Stepping forward without preparation can be daunting ... so prepare, but never let preparation turn into procrastination. The goal is to step forward. Show your interest in a role or an assignment.

2. **Be conscious**

Be aware of what is going on around you. What are the opportunities, the threats, the agendas and the politics in operation in your firm? This is not Machiavellian, it is wise.

Think broadly and engage your network. What are the roles and assignments that are available in the firm? What are the advantages and disadvantages of each?

3. **Be prepared to give yourself the time you need to prepare and a deadline**

   If you need time to prepare, know that about yourself and carve out that time in your diary together with deadlines. Reflect on the things that are holding you back from the list above and use your analytical and networking skills to prepare a plan that allows you to step forward with confidence and clarity.

4. **Be aware of 'the other'**

   Being offered a role or assignment — Remember that the person asking you to consider a role is unaware of the internal monologue going on in your head. They may perceive your hesitation and need for reflection as a lack of enthusiasm. If you need time to think but are interested, tell them that — remember framing from Chapter 9. Do not explain all of the reasons why you think you might not be the right person even if that is going through your head — remember disclosure from Chapter 9. Think about how what you want to say will land with them.

   Stepping forward to volunteer for a role or assignment — This should ideally not come out of the blue. Give the other person time to think. Women I have worked with have come back from programmes they have found inspirational and marched into the partner's office and announced for the first time that they want to be a partner. What has then ensued is that the partner, taken by surprise, says something mildly discouraging like 'we didn't know you were interested in that and will need to look at our plans' or 'I am not sure you are ready for that step', resulting in a downspin in the woman. If she had given the partner the 'heads up' that she wanted to talk about her career and potential career trajectory he could have looked at his plans and thought about what she needed to do to be on track for partnership.

If you have talked about your career aspirations and interests in your appraisal (Chapter 17) and had regular catch-up discussions about what you have been doing (Chapter 8) you are preparing those around you, and yourself, for the point where you step forward.

5. Step forward
Do it!

Exercise
Consider what more you could be stepping forward for in your firm:

• What advantages to you would that step bring?

• What is holding you back?

○ Internally — your own fears

○ Externally — the firm's set-up or situations at home

- How could you overcome these barriers?

- What support do you need?

- What is the first step?

My Challenges to You

Prepare and then step forward — you and your career deserve it.

Tips from the top — Advice from partners to women in their firm

'Plan prepare and practice ... and then do it'.

'Believe in yourself — if you don't you can't expect others to'.

'Plan but be flexible, be prepared to take the opportunities as they arise'.

'You need to say what you want'.

'Don't beat yourself up about not being good enough'.

'Be prepared to get out of your comfort zone and try out some other things'.

'Be prepared to be flexible and to take risks'.

'Ask yourself — Would a man in your position hold back?'.

'Speak up. Most partners are proud when you shine'.

'Have patience and keep going'.

'Ask for forgiveness not permission'.

RESOURCES

Kay, K., & Shipman, C. (2014). The confidence gap. *The Atlantic Magazine*, May 2014.

Saujani, R. Teach girls bravery not perfection. TED talk.

Mohr, T. (2015). Helping an employee overcome their self-doubt. *Harvard Business Review*, October.

(This article looks at imposter syndrome and the inner critic from the manager's point of view which is illuminating.)

Sandberg, S. (2013). *Lean in: Women, work, and the will to lead*. London: WH Allen.

CHAPTER 11

WHO KNOWS WHAT YOU DO — EFFECTIVE AND EFFICIENT NETWORKING

Networking takes up my precious time. I was employed for the quality of my brain not to stand in some large room with a bunch of strangers whilst balancing a glass of wine and a plate of food and trying desperately to think of something to say. I would rather be at home, I would rather be working, I would rather be doing anything else.

— Senior Manager of a big four firm

I have never worked with anybody, male or female, who loves this kind of a large business networking event, but networking is vital, does not only happen at 'events' and it can be enjoyable. Being good, or even the best, at what you do is necessary but not sufficient; others also need to know about what you offer and that is where networking comes in. The good news is that if you are strategic about your networking it does not need to take up much time, nor does it need to be awkward and you can avoid unproductive, time wasting moments in large networking events.

Networking happens all the time, from these large events to casual conversations in the office. To save your time and energy and achieve what you want, you do need to be strategic about the networking you do. This does not mean being Machiavellian or manipulative; it simply means thinking through what you want and how you can achieve this most effectively so that your precious time is spent productively. My suggestion is that you spend a little more time planning and following up and a lot less time in large events. The good news is that the research suggests that women are excellent at making connections socially; the bad news is that they are less good at using the connections they make at work strategically to achieve their goals.

In Chapter 3 I talked about your support network. These are the people at home and at work who can make life easier for you; this chapter concentrates on a more strategic network. The tips in this chapter can also be used to develop your support network, but here I will be concentrating on your strategic network, the network that can give you opportunities inside and outside your firm.

Networking at work is about giving and receiving information. This is an area where you are not simply the expert in your subject; you are investigating other people's worlds to gather information. Asking questions and listening are key skills, but you do also need to be able to talk about what you do.

Why is networking important?

- Expanding opportunities for you and for the firm:
  - By knowing what others are doing
  - By them knowing what you do
- It is part of being politically wise and effective:
  - Understanding the real agendas
  - Understanding where the real power lies
  - Understanding the alliances
- Developing rewarding relationships:
  - New ones
  - Maintaining and refreshing existing ones
- Others are doing it — and getting the rewards

In this chapter I am going to pose the key questions first and I suggest that you think very specifically about your situation rather than reading this as a theoretical piece. The key questions are why, what, who and how. I am going to expand on the 'how' to cover the three broad opportunities you have to network and how you can get the most effective outcome for your input of time from every opportunity.

KEY QUESTIONS FOR YOU

Why Should You Carve Out Precious Time to Network?

The first key step is to **be clear about your goal** — what it is that you want to accomplish from this networking. Is it:

- being in the best position to advance your career and achieve your potential?

- getting to work on a particular project?

- winning work from external clients?

What Do You Need People in Your Network to Know about You?

The second step is to **be clear about what you offer and what you are interested in.** Your exploration of what you offer from Chapter 4 and the short speech in Chapter 8 about what you do is the start. This is not about 'blowing your own trumpet'; it is telling people what they need to know to make informed decisions about you and your work.

Who Needs to Know about You in Order to Achieve Your Goals?

Exercise
The next step is to take a blank piece of paper and **plot your network**. The network will be different depending on the goal, but in each case put yourself in the middle

and think broadly about who can help you accomplish your goal. If you know them draw the connections (as shown with a, b and c), if you don't already know them then they are floating (y and z).

Who is in your current network?

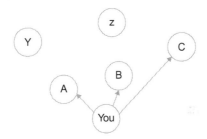

If the goal is to be in the best position to advance your career, the people you need to have in the map are the people who will be making decisions on your career. Are you clear about who the decision makers are? They may not be in your office or in your service line or even in your country. There may also be key influencers who do not have positional power but can influence those that do. Do you know who they are? What are the alliances and patterns of influence between the people on your map?

When you have drawn your map share it with others to check that you have identified the key players and their connections.

Exercise
Who knows what about you?

Once you have a clear idea of the key players it is time to get into the detail of the current position:

Who are the individuals who have power over your career?	How do you interact with them?	What is their opinion of you?	Do they know what you want from your career?

What gaps does this analysis reveal?

What do you need to change?

The same strategy applies if the goal is to get onto a particular project. Use your existing knowledge and network to ensure you know who the decision makers and influencers are and then think carefully about what they know about you and your suitability for the project.

If the goal is to win business, your map is likely to include people inside and outside your firm. The unconnected people may be targets or people in your firm who you don't know but have connections to your targets. Ensure that those on the map include past clients. Often we move on to the next project without a backward glance at the clients we were working with who would be really good advocates for us and our work. It does not matter what level they are, they all have some influence within their organisation. Think also of your wider social circle. This is often an awkward one, I am wary of advocating 'selling' to friends, but simply ensure they do know what work you do and are interested in. It would be a travesty if they went to a competitor or did not mention you simply out of ignorance.

How Are You Going to Make the Connections?

Think about how you can connect with those on your internal and external maps in ways that are authentic and move you towards your goal.

Internally

If your goal is advancing your career you may need to reconnect with those that already know you (a, b and c in my network map above) to ensure that they have a recent and accurate view of what you have been up to, and what you are interested in. It is worth thinking about how many influential people in your organisation would talk about you as the junior they worked with 5 years ago rather than the woman you are now?

You may need to ask those that already know you to make introductions to others (y and z). Most will be very happy to facilitate this if you give a reasoned argument about why you need that contact or what is in it for the other party.

If the reason is to ensure you are known by influential decision makers in your firm so that they can make informed decisions about your career then you have options as to how you frame the need for contact:

1. Find a reason that it might be useful for them to know about you and the work you do. Think broadly on this one — clients in common, targets you are interested in, work that they may be interested in but are unaware of.

2. Ask them for advice. If you are looking for promotion and they are more senior are there things that they can give you advice on? Advice is a powerful connector; not only will it give you useful information, but it also will link you to the other person who now knows about you and your goal.

3. Ask an existing contact to talk to them about you and the work you do so that the other party is informed by somebody they know and trust. Often this is the role of the sponsor — see Chapter 12.

Externally

If the reason for making contact is to develop your business externally, think broadly and use all the resources available to you within the firm. Are there business development professionals in the firm that could give you support in investigating the target or making the contact? Have you used the client databases available to you in the firm to investigate who else in the firm has contacts at the target that they could use to introduce you?

If you involve others in the firm in your clients they are often more willing to bring you along to their meetings, allowing you to cross sell.

What Are the Available Opportunities to Network?

I think at this stage it is worth being very specific about how you can get the best of the networking opportunities you have. There are broadly three opportunities to network:

- Everyday conversations
- Networking events
- Specific networking conversations

  I will take these in turn.

Everyday Conversations at Work

There are two elements to consider in these conversations: the task and the relationship. In most circumstances we concentrate on the task, allowing the person to think of us only in relation to that task.

It is worth considering whether it is appropriate to take the conversation beyond the task; 'what else are you working on?' is a good opener as is 'how is business going?'. Most people are very happy to give you more information about what and how they are doing and will ask you what you are working on. This gives you the chance to bring in your work interests (which you have thought through as a result of the work in Chapter 8 and can give a BEST response) so that they see you as somebody who has an existence and interests beyond the current task. This is true whether the other person is inside or outside your firm.

The innocuous question at the office coffee machine 'how are you?' can be answered in a number of ways and it is worth being mindful of the impact these might have. We explored this in Chapter 8, and to remind you there are some subtexts that go with some of the more common responses:

'Fine' = don't ask any more about me.

'Really busy' = don't think about approaching me with any of your interesting work or questions as I am overloaded.

'Stressed' = I can't cope with the work load I already have so please don't give me any more work or questions no matter how interesting it is.

Alternatively, you can give a BEST response along the lines of 'I am good. I have been working on a really interesting project that I think could have some useful implications for the work we do in X sector which is growing. How are you?'. This gives a mental link between you and this project and sector. You are available both for interesting work in this area and for answering questions about it.

Networking Events

These can be awkward, enjoyable social times or great opportunities to move towards your goal. Much can be gained by the small talk over the finger food, but they are a productive use of your time if you are guided by these rules:

Before the event

1. Be clear about why you are going. What specific outcome would make this a successful event for you? If you do not have a desired outcome don't go!

2. When you accept the invitation put half an hour in your diary a few days before the event to prepare and connect prior to the event and half an hour the morning after to follow up.

3. Get hold of the guest list. Identify three people who are going who you would like to connect with to meet your goal. Rank them in order of importance.

4. Consider sending an email to the top ranked person, saying that you are delighted they are going and wondering if they might be free for a coffee before the event (depending on their seniority and your relationship). Very often the other person will also be dreading the event and will be delighted to have a brief conversation and somebody to walk in with, so will accept your invitation.

5. Consider sending the other two contacts emails to say that you see they are going to the event and say that you are hoping to see them there. This gives you the opening to contact them afterwards if you do not see them at the event.

6. Review the LinkedIn (or other professional networking platform) profiles of interesting attendees to gather background information; see who else in your firm knows them well so that they can introduce you and help you avoid faux pas.

7. Ensure your LinkedIn profile says what you want it to say — people will meet you and then look you up.

8. Identify somebody from your firm who is also going and would work with you at the event — your buddy. Understand what you both want to get from the event and how you can help each other.

9. Ensure your business cards are in your pocket.

10. Think about how you talk about what you do (see Chapter 8).

During the event

1. Remember that all attendees are there to network and are as keen as you are. You will be interesting to them as a contact. Think about how you can help them, this is often a much more useful mindset than thinking you are there to sell.

2. You are not at the event as an expert that is expected to know all the answers. Ask open questions about their business and listen carefully to see how you can easily help them.

3. Be prepared to talk engagingly about what you do — that is why you are both there. They do want to know about you and your work.

4. Do not see a friend and spend the rest of the evening talking to them or others that you are regularly in contact with unless this is your goal from the event.

5. Work with your buddy:

    a. Rescue each other from conversations that are going on too long 'sorry to interrupt but can I just borrow you as I need to introduce you to X' works well and causes no offence.

    b. Open up groups you are talking to so that your buddy can join and you can then move on.

6. Do not be afraid to leave early if you have achieved what you want to — this is your evening.

After the event

1. Write down one fact about the people you met on the back of their business cards on the way home while they are still fresh in your mind (not if you are driving!).

2. Use the time you have set aside the next morning to send emails and record who you met. Think about what you can personalise and send them from the firm's publications.

3. Record the contacts on the firm's client contact database.

4. Contact those internally who have also recorded these people as contacts so that they are aware of the connection and of you.

5. Put half an hour in your diary as a recurring feature every month and use that time to review your contacts list and think about what they might be interested in. Use the information you picked up at the event. Aim to send them something that they will be interested in every quarter and always personalise it to show why you think they might be interested.

SPECIFIC NETWORKING CONVERSATIONS

Networking during everyday conversations and at networking events are usually done; but often not done well. Specific networking conversations are often not done at all by women. Partners remark that men will come in and tell them about the work they are doing, but they are not approached by the women at the same level and have to search them out.

I am not suggesting random conversations with people you do not know and have no connections with. I am suggesting well thought through conversations with somebody where you are clear what is in it for them as well as what you want to get out of it.

Step one: Clarity about what you are trying to achieve

Is this about winning work – ensuring that those who make decisions about where work is placed internally and externally know what you offer?

Alternatively, are you ensuring that those who will make decisions about your career are doing this with the advantage of knowing who you are and what you do?

Step two: Identification

Look at your network map. Who are the key players? If you know them, do they have the information that you would wish them to have? This is different from 'they should know' or 'if they bothered to ask around they would have the information'. The question is if they were asked (as you hope they will be) would they be able to easily recall the information you would want them to?

Most senior people do not have the time to search you out, but often they would find it really useful to know what you are doing. Turn it around and think about your juniors. Do you have the time to search them out and ask them to explain what they are up to beyond the tasks that you know about? Wouldn't it be useful every now and again if they came to you and talked you through what they are up to in a time efficient way? The same applies to the more senior people you work with.

Step three: Finding the link

What do you know about the person you have identified? It is worth looking them up on the internal system and looking at them on LinkedIn. The link between you is usually a person, a client, a common interest or all three (**Figure 11.1**).

Figure 11.1: Finding the Link.

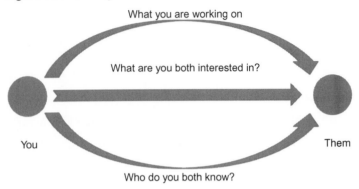

Who do you know who knows the person you want to talk to? Look at your network. Is there somebody in your current network who could make the introduction or who could pass on information? If there is such a person the question becomes 'does that connection have the relevant information about you and why would they expend their energy to pass it on?'. What could you do to help them? The first and obvious answer is to ask them, but this may not be easy and you might need to think carefully about what is in it for them to help you. If you have an active sponsor (see Chapter 12) this is often their role, but others are surprisingly willing to help if you ask.

Could you talk to them about something that you are both interested in or working on? Internally your career is always something that partners are interested in and they will be interested in giving advice.

Step four: Identifying the benefit

What is the benefit to the person identified of talking to you? What information do you have that they would be interested in? They may have the information if they had the time to look, but actually having a conversation with you might be the most efficient way of getting that information.

If the link is a client, the question you need to ask yourself is what benefit will the person get from hearing the information you hold about the client — what is the advantage for them of having the conversation with you?

The same is true if the link is a common interest.

Step five: Asking for the conversation

Once you are clear about the advantage to the other person it is much easier to make the contact and invite them to talk to you. This is no longer a conversation that only you want but a conversation that you both will benefit from.

The most difficult thing is asking — just do it. Others are doing it and they are reaping the rewards. As Marianne Williamson (and Nelson Mandela) say 'Your playing small does not serve the world'; and it certainly does not serve you!

MY CHALLENGES TO YOU

1. Take networking seriously. Put time in your diary to plan for it and then do it.

2. Remember you cannot make others do what you want them to do, but if they do not have the information you have and they need, you cannot blame them for making ill-informed decisions.

3. Give yourself a target for the next month:

   ○ Who are you going to make contact with?

   ○ What do you need to do to get ready for this contact?

Tips from the top — Advice from partners to women in their firm

'Networking is an important part of work and should be seen as such'.

'Find out who is influential and find a reason to talk to them'.

'People like to be asked for advice'.

'Walk a different way to the coffee machine and pop into the partners' offices as you do'.

'You need a 'board' of people who can help you and you need to ask for that help'.

'Build your network from above, below and among your peers — you need them all'.

'Clients are people too. They want to engage with you, after all you are a good person *and* you have something to offer in both your expertise and your connections in the firm'.

'Think about what you can do to help solve their problem, whatever it is'.

RESOURCE

Sole, D., & Roberts, B. (2015). *21st Century networking*. Elliot & Thompson Ltd.

CHAPTER 12

SPONSORSHIP: THE SHARP END OF YOUR DEVELOPMENTAL NETWORK

*We should always have three friends in our
lives — one who walks ahead who we look up to
and follow; one who walks beside us, who is with
us every step of our journey; and then, one who
we reach back for and bring along after we've
cleared the way.*

— Michelle Obama

In many ways our working lives in professional service
firms echo our lives at university and school where
women do so well; intelligence is paramount. As with our
academic institutions we are told the firm is a meritocracy. However, like Alice through the looking glass the
working world looks the same but the rules are funda-
mentally different.

The reality is that you need a sponsor. Not to replace
the hard work and successes, but to ensure that they are
noticed and acted upon. Senior partners I have talked to
notice that men are sponsored more actively than women.

To a large extent the issue here is an organisational one and I absolutely believe that firms need to help women by offering sponsorship; however you need to know what you need, so that you can look out for it and ask for it.

FIRST STEP — ROLES IN YOUR DEVELOPMENTAL NETWORK, A PURIST'S GUIDE

Think carefully about your network. Look back at Chapter 11 and identify who takes the following roles in your network. Often partners around you play more than one role but I am going to be purist here and separate out the roles so that you can see what is needed and what is compromised when partners take more than one role.

APPRAISING PARTNER

This is an organisational role. This partner will see you probably once a year to talk through your appraisal and development. They are interested in your work and will look backwards at your performance and forward at your goals. Politically you need to be conscious about what you say to this partner as they have power over your performance ratings and pay. Think carefully about what you disclose and how you frame what you say.

You will be given an appraising partner by the firm. For more information on how to use your meetings with that person, please turn to Chapter 17.

SUPPORTERS

This is not an organisational role; rather it is a role that partners and other senior people you work with will offer you if they think that you are good. Supporters are interested in your work and what you can offer the firm, but they are not putting their reputation on the line for you. It is good to have as many supporters as you can. Like the appraising partner you need to be conscious about what you say to your supporters as they have a vested interest in you staying with the firm and working hard for and with them.

You will earn supporters by doing really good work. They may talk about what you have done to others in the natural course of discussions, but do not be shy about explicitly asking them to talk about what you have done for them so that others are also aware.

You will not be able to work for very many partners because you will not have the time or the network, but you can also gain supporters by giving internal presentations and engaging with those around you at all levels. Talking about what you do will gain you supporters if you do it in a way that shows you off to your BEST — see Chapter 8.

MENTORS

This can be either an informal or a formal role. What you need from a mentor is a sounding board, a gate opener and a view from the outside. The focus is on you and your life, taking a longer and broader perspective to the other roles. Your mentor should be impartial. The acid test is that a true mentor might advise you to think about other jobs; your appraising partner and your supporters are unlikely to do that as they have a vested interest in you working for them and for the firm. Because a true mentor does not have any personal stake in you staying and working for the firm you can tell them anything and you do not need to be conscious about what you disclose or how you frame things.

Acquiring a mentor is not simple. My advice is to think firstly about what you want from them and jot down an informal 'job description'. Once you are clear about what you want think broadly about your network. I often find that old bosses make good mentors; they know you well and are no longer line managing you. You may want somebody outside your group or service line or even outside the firm. Keep looking for them; it may be that you get what you need from a combination of people. Often senior people are prepared to give you time and thought if you do all the arranging; they see it as paying back the time and attention they got from their own mentors. Be prepared to ask and be clear about what you are looking for from them.

SPONSOR

This is a role like no other. The key differentiator is that the sponsor is prepared to risk their reputation on you. They will step forward and tell others how good you are and that they think you deserve a promotion. They will talk about you to others, introduce you to those who you need to know and work with you to influence those that are not yet on your side. Their role includes ensuring you are given the work that will show you off and helping you to navigate the politics.

Because the relationship is reciprocal (you give them excellent work and they work on your behalf) you need to ensure that you make them look good and that there are no surprises. They do need you to be excellent so that their judgement is not questioned.

A sponsor needs to believe in you and the more energy, power and influence they have, the better. How you get a sponsor differs between all the firms I have worked with. In some you are allocated a sponsor, in others you will need to ask who would be the most appropriate sponsor, in others the relationship develops organically over time. The key thing is to know what the role is and look out for somebody who could play that role for you.

What your sponsor needs from you to do their job effectively is the following:

1. Excellent work so that their judgement in sponsoring you does not reflect badly on them

2. Information and regular updates about what you offer the firm so that they can talk about you and the work you are doing in an informed way (see Chapter 4)

3. Assurance that you want to progress in the organisation so that it is worth them putting their energy into helping you (see Chapter 5)

4. What your USP is (see Chapter 8)

5. You want to make them look good

Figure 12.1: The Different Roles in Your Development.

	Appraising Partner	Supporter	Mentor	Sponsor
Direction of interest	What the firm gets from you	What they can give to you	What they can give to you	Reciprocal
Area of interest	Your work	You	You	Your promotion
Time scale	Year on year	Medium term	Long term	Medium term
Personal stake	Yes	Yes	No	Yes
What you want	Feedback Honesty	Belief in you	Introductions Advice Overview Sounding board	Feedback Honesty Belief in you Introductions Advice Overview Sounding board Presents you Represents you Protects you Influence Prepared to risk their reputation on you
What they want from you	You to do your job well	You to shine	You to fulfil your potential	Stellar performance
Disclosure required	Consciously think about what you disclose and how you frame your interactions	Consciously think about what you disclose and how you frame your interactions	Full – because they have no personal stake	Consciously think about what you disclose and how you frame your interactions

MIXED ROLES, THE REALITY

In the world of professional service firms these roles may not be as purely delineated as I have described above and one person may do more than one role, but you need each of these roles to be taken on by somebody. Women are often seen to be good at getting mentors and supporters, but not as good at getting or using sponsors (**Figure 12.1**).

WHAT ARE THE DANGERS?

Not being aware of the need for active sponsorship can lead you to be overlooked. It is a vital role and I have seen women fail to be considered for promotion and even one fail in a promotion process because her sponsor was not active on her behalf.

Women are often judged harshly if they step forward and promote themselves directly and as a result many find it uncomfortable to do so. Some women do not have access to the informal networks that operate at work during male social events with or without clients. The result is that women are hampered by what is acceptable for women and an absence of the informal view of what is happening at the firm. This means that having a sponsor is particularly important for women.

Finding a sponsor is not only particularly important, but also more challenging for women. This is the case for a number of reasons:

• Women are not offered sponsorship in the way that men are. This may be because of the very human desire to sponsor a 'mini-me', somebody who reminds us of ourselves at an earlier stage in our career. Because of the high proportion of male partners in firms men are more likely to be seen as a 'mini-me' and sponsored.

- Sponsorship is often an activity that takes place outside of the office working environment, the 'tips of the trade' are passed on in ad hoc conversations rather than in formal or work-related situations. Some male partners may feel it unnatural and inappropriate to engage in the same social activities with female staff as they do with the men who work with them. The activities of going out for a drink after work or watching men play sport are laden with additional subtle nuances if you are a male partner taking a female junior. Some partners find it easier to avoid the situation than to think about how they might deal with the additional questions it raises if the junior is female.

My challenge here is primarily to your firm and the partners within it to step forward and ensure that women are offered the same quality of sponsorship as their male peers, but there are things that we can do as women.

MY TOP TIPS ARE

- Ask for what you need. If you do not feel comfortable asking for a sponsor directly, ask for advice as to who would be the best sponsor for you, setting out what you need and why.

- Do not rely on one sponsor. Ensure your development network is rich in depth and breadth, so that if your sponsor leaves you are not stranded. Do you have sup-porters who would become sponsors in these circumstances?

- Sponsor the women who work for you and you think have the potential to progress in the firm. As Madeline Albright famously said *there is a special place in hell for women who do not help other women*. I am not suggesting that you do not sponsor the good men too, but please ensure the good women below you are getting the sponsorship that they need.

MY CHALLENGES TO YOU

1. Identify who takes each of these roles in your development network

   - Sponsor

   - Supporters

   - Appraising partner

   - Mentor

2. Ensure that they have the information they need to perform their role

---

Tips from the top — Advice from partners to women in their firm

'Your sponsor is vital. I couldn't have achieved what I have done without a sponsor'.

'Ensure your sponsor is doing their job for you. They need information and access to your plan. You need to work together as a team'.

'Ask for what you need, including that partners will protect you'.

'Have your own informal board of directors, ask for advice and use them'.

'Use the support of those who want you to progress'.

'The partners that had supported me left whilst I was on maternity leave and this caused a problem. It is important to have a range of supporters and keep in contact with them'.

'I had two mentors, one was inside the firm and one was outside'.

'Be prepared to ask for help, it is not a weakness. You cannot drive a career on your own'.

'Ensure you know the difference between a sponsor and a mentor and have a sponsor who will speak up for you'.

'My sponsor was good at challenging me — he asked me why I was not going for partnership'.

'You have to move your career forward. People are very willing to help, but you need to ask for that help'.

RESOURCES

Hewlett, S. A. (2013). Forget a mentor find a sponsor — The new way to fast track your career. *Harvard Business Review Press*.

Ibarra, H., Carter, N. M., & Silva, C. (2010). Why men still get more promotions than women. *Harvard Business Review*, September.

CHAPTER 13

ROLE MODELS

We do not imitate, but are a model to others'
— Pericles

As women we look around for role models within our firm. Typically we are looking for more senior women in our firm who have made similar life choices to ours. This means that we are looking for female partners who are probably in the same technical area as us and have made the same decisions about their families as we have, or would wish to do in the future. Consequently we are looking at a very small group of women, hence the 'problem' with finding role models.

I have talked to a number of women who leave firms because of their perceived lack of role models. They think it is not possible to do what they want to do in their firm because nobody has done it before in exactly that way. They are looking for a woman exactly like them in an already small pool of female partners. This is making life unnecessarily difficult. The 'lack of role models' played

an important part in my leaving PwC and I wish somebody had challenged me about this view at the time.

There is evidence to suggest that men choose their role
models in a different way. They also look around their firm
for role models, but instead of expecting one person to
embody all that they want to be, they 'cherry pick' from
what they see as the best of the best around them and use
the best bits of those around them to create a composite
role model. This makes it much easier as they have more
choice. We can learn something from the men here.

Exercise

In order to turn this finding into a practical tool, can I
suggest you start looking at role models from the other
end? Rather than looking at what is out there in your
firm, consider what kind of leader you want to be. Write
down the adjectives that you would wish to embody in
the first column of the following table:

The leader I want to be:	Who does this in a way I admire?	What exactly do they do?
e.g., Strategic thinker		

(*Continued*)

The leader I want to be:	Who does this in a way I admire?	What exactly do they do?

Review the adjectives. Are they what you really want to be at work? Are they a development from who you already are? Review them in the light of the feedback you have had. My tip in this review is that they should be a stretch progression from where you are, but not trying to be a totally different person.

Once you are happy with the description of the leader you want to be in the first column look carefully around you. Who excels at each of the things you want to be? Put their names in the second column. Don't chose somebody like Nelson Mandela; you haven't actually seen him operate and it is easy to project all kinds of things onto such distant role models. Chose somebody that you have seen doing what you would like to do.

The sum of this second column is your composite role model. You will be a leader unlike any of the leaders around you because you are a different person, but you want to embody what you see as the best mix of their characteristics. You may find that some of what you want is not displayed by a partner, but by a peer or a junior; you can learn from them in just the same way and they can certainly be part of your composite role model.

The next step is to think about how they actually do what they do. If you are not close enough to be absolutely clear you will need to ask them about it. Show them that you are working on your development and would like some practical advice about how they do what they do in the area you admire. From these observations and conversations start to fill in the third column.

This table now articulates what you aspire to and where you see it in practice. I suggest you use it as a developing tool to articulate and formulate what you are aiming for and how you have seen it done. In this way the role models around you contribute in a rich and fertile way to your development.

What you are now describing is the leader you would like to be which is not exactly like any existing leader, which is an advantage, but is practical and rooted in the reality of what you have seen work. Be prepared to talk about those aspirations as part of your development discussions (see Chapter 17).

WOMEN ASSESSING OTHER WOMEN

In all the development programmes I run I ask a number of partners (predominately female but also male) from the firm to come and talk to younger women. I have recorded the tips that they gave throughout the book in the section at the end of the chapter called 'Tips from the top'. I have been very aware of how harshly the female partners and their choices are judged by the women I am working with. This is the other side of expecting to find a single perfect role model; when real women around us do not match up to this perfect ideal in all aspects of their lives we can be very judgemental. Remember to only take what you value from each of the 'role models' around you, nobody is perfect.

Their choices may not be ours but we can learn from them, and particularly the elements we admire, without damming them for the elements that we do not value and the choices we would not make.

MY CHALLENGES TO YOU

Challenge your thinking about role models.

1. Consider the composite elements of the leader you aspire to be, who around you does this and how do they do it.

2. Learn from those whose ways of working you admire whether they are male or female, not to become a copy, but to become the best you can be by learning from the best around you. Note it down when you see behaviour that you particularly admire

> **Tips from the top — Advice from partners to women in their firm**
>
> 'Pick different aspects from your role models using as wide a pool as possible'.
>
> 'Don't judge other women. We are all doing what works for us'.

RESOURCE

Ibarra, H. (2015). The authenticity paradox. *Harvard Business Review*, January.

CHAPTER 14

FINDING YOUR EQUILIBRIUM

Nothing ever fatigues me but doing what I do not like

— Jane Austen, Mansfield Park

This chapter is about how you want to fit all the things that are important to you into your life. These might include:

- Your major relationships with family and friends
- Children
- Hobbies
- Time to recharge your batteries
- Work that gives you stimulation and reward

Your list may well be longer, but you will see this is not a work/life balance issue; it is an issue of finding your equilibrium. The equilibrium that gives you what you want in sustainable and enjoyable quantities.

Many young women leave professional service firms in their late twenties and early thirties; indeed for many

firms this is the point where the female attrition rates are
at their highest when compared with their male peers.
The reason often given for a move at this stage is to find
a role with better work—life equilibrium.

For some this is the move to prepare for the potential
of being a mother. These women are not pregnant, they
often do not yet have life partners, but they do feel that it
would be impossible to raise a family in the way they
want to and do the work required if they were more
senior in the firm. Others are not planning on being
mothers but have interests outside work that they see as
being incompatible with the hours partners work. This is
the position of many male and female millennials and
firms are starting to see a move away from an acceptance
of delayed gratification. This poses a challenge to the traditional business model of professional service firms
which requires long hours to prove your worth on the
promise of becoming a partner.

I totally understand this and moved from audit to take
a role in the tax department of PwC at this point in my
career for these very reasons. Perhaps you too are thinking about changing role within the firm or moving outside the firm to find a role that is more compatible with
getting your equilibrium now and in the future. If so, this
is the chapter for you.

WHAT IS YOUR EQUILIBRIUM?

The right equilibrium will be different for every person.
The key thing is to get the balance between all the elements in your life that is right for you. Enough of what

you love at work and enough of what you love at home. Whether you are thinking of having children or not the balance you want will change as you (and they) grow and develop.

In Chapter 3 we explored how you can keep up your energy levels in a normal working week which is an important part of the story, but the scary and vital question that motivates many women to move roles or organisations is 'will I be able to maintain my equilibrium if I am a partner with all the additional pressures that commensurate with that role?'.

WHAT DOES IT TAKE TO BE A SUCCESSFUL PARTNER?

In order to find and maintain your equilibrium you first need to be sure about what is needed to give you satisfaction in each of the constituent parts of your life. For many of the women I work with the element that is perceived to expand to make other parts impossible to fit in is a senior role in a professional service firm, so let us take a good look at the perceptions and reality of what is expected of you as a partner. I am going to talk about the role of a partner, but if it is more appropriate to look at a less senior role please do substitute the name of that role for my references to partnership.

In 2012, Mckinsey & Co undertook some research in the United Kingdom with thousands of women who worked for professional service firms and found that the vast majority of women looked at the partners around them and believe that to become a partner work has to be their number one priority. Seventy-one per cent of the women sampled agreed with the statement that to make it to partner 'Work must be the number one priority' against only 59% of the men, despite the fact that the men and women worked for the same organisations. It is clear from this that there is no obvious consensus as to what role partnership has to take in your life if you are to make it to partner and that, in the United Kingdom at least, men have a rather different perception of what it takes to become a partner (McKinsey 30% club & YSC, 2012, shifting the needle).

There are often three partner 'job descriptions' in circulation among the women I work with:

1. My current perception of what a partner has to do

2. The reality of what is expected of a partner

3. What I would do as a partner

DUE DILIGENCE – CHECKING OUT WHAT YOU THINK YOU KNOW

If you don't fancy job description number 1 because it would not give you time for the other things you want to do, you need to check that your perceptions are right. Do some due diligence by talking to a number of partners you know well and others in your network to understand:

• Do they enjoy their role as partner?

• What are the things that they enjoy inside and outside work?

• How do they get time to do the things outside of work that they want to do in their lives?

- Is there any appetite within the firm to do partnership differently?

The partners I talk to are clear that there are additional challenges to being a partner, but there are also huge rewards in terms of autonomy. Not only the autonomy to build the business you want to build for your team, but also the autonomy to run your life in the way that works for you, your family and your business. We are quick to judge others about the life choices they make, but they are different and the choices they make about how they deal with their lives and their children are active decisions that work for their situation. My suggestion is that you learn from them and then make your own decisions about what will work for you.

I also hear subtly different perceptions of what is required of a partner within the same firm. This is confusing but also reveals some flexibility to create the partner role that you are interested in – job description number 3.

WHAT IS AVAILABLE TO YOU IN TERMS OF INFORMATION FROM THE FIRM?

Check out job description number 2. Is there anything available to you from within the firm that states what is expected of partners? You might want to talk to HR and the partners around you to ascertain what is available.

WHAT TYPE OF LEADER DO YOU WANT TO BE?

Having done your due diligence and understood what you can about what will be required of you as a partner, it is important that you think through what you would offer as job description number 3, the partner you would want to be:

Exercise

- What would give you energy about having the role of partner in your firm?

- What are the aspects of the role that drain your energy when you think of them?

- How would you create your equilibrium?

  - What are the activities that give you energy and you want to ensure you have time for? (See Chapter 3)

- How could you structure your day/week/year, so that you can ensure you have time for these activities?

- How could you minimise the aspects of the role that you see as energy draining?

- What are you prepared to offer the firm? How would you structure your working life to ensure equilibrium for you?

- What is in it for them? What makes you special and somebody that they are prepared to accommodate in the way you want to work (see Chapter 4)? How would you describe to them the advantages of having you as the partner working in the way you want to work?

- What more do you need to do to make this a compelling proposition for the firm?

Ultimately if the offer from you, both in terms of what you bring and how you want to work as a partner, is not sufficiently compelling for the firm and they can only contemplate something that does not work for you, then you do not want that role and partnership at this firm is not for you. But you owe it to yourself and the partnership to ensure what you want is not possible before you leave. Leaving because you do not think it is possible to be the kind of partner you want to be, but have not thoroughly checked this out is an opportunity lost for both you and the firm.

MY CHALLENGES TO YOU

Check out your perceptions of what partners do and why they do the job they do against the reality of their experience.

1. Check out what is known about what your firm requires of its partners.

2. Think about the senior role you want to take in the firm and how you would structure that to maintain your equilibrium.

3. Talk to others about what they think of what you are offering – your mentor will be really useful in this examination.

4. Start to explore what is possible in your firm.

Tips from the top — advice from partners to women in their firm

'Challenge your own assumptions about what is possible'.

'You need to be clear about what kind of partner you will be'.

'Have some clear rules about what is important to you and stick to them'.

'The hardest time for me was being the level below partner when you have responsibility with less autonomy or control'.

'If you are going to work flexibly it is important that you know what your boundaries are, communicate them and stick to them'.

'It is a partnership and we work together. You will be supported in a different way as a fellow partner, but the support will be there for you'.

'As a partner you can manage your life, and your time more easily, and organise your juniors' lives at work around you'.

'When you get pregnant is not important to your career but it is important to your life. Where you are in your career should not be a factor in when you try for a baby. You can make maternity leave work at any stage of your career and there is no ideal time. Partnership is about the long term, not the short term'.

'Having a child is not mutually exclusive with career success. I thought they would think I was not serious about my career if I had children, and I was scared to go and say I was pregnant. I realised I created many of these problems in my mind'.

'My role as a mother is important, I needed to miss my first partners meeting because my child needed me, and I was very scared about doing this. I talked to the partners and explained that I wanted to be a good professional, but I also needed to be a good mother. They understood'.

'You are a perfectionist and there are days when you will feel you don't do a job well either in the home or the office. Don't judge yourself on a day by day basis, just don't make the same mistake two days running'.

'You do not need to be perfect as a mother or as a partner within the firm'.

'Know what is important to you in looking after your children. This may be by being there for bath times, or being there in the morning. But your way of doing it will be different from everybody else. There is no perfect way, there is only the right way for you and your family'.

'I can be a super mum one day, a super worker another and a super lover on another day. I can't be all of those things on the same day!'.

'Find the balance that you are comfortable with'.

'Invest in yourself — time, fun, cosmetics, clothes ... whatever you enjoy'.

'Take care of yourself and your career'.

'There are four pillars in my life and I make time to attend to and enjoy all of them:

- Health

- Relationships

- Work

- Finances'.

'Keep your focus and make conscious choices'.

'Be selfish at times — it is in everybody's long term interest that you are strategically selfish periodically'.

'Keep to your boundaries so that your work suits you'.

'I made decisions at a time that suited me'.

'Find the working pattern that works for you — we are not brain surgeons and nobody will die'.

RESOURCES

Reid, E. Why we pretend to be workaholics. *HBR Ideacast.*

Shipman, C., & Kay, K. (2010). *Womenomics: Work less, achieve more, live better.* HarperCollins Publishers.

McKinsey 30% club & YSC. (2012). Shifting the needle.

Meers, S., & Strober, J. (2013). *Getting to 50/50, how working parents can have it all.* Viva Editions.

Mohr, T. (2015). *Playing Big: A practical guide for brilliant women like you.* London: Penguin Random House.

CHAPTER 15

BEING COMMERCIAL

When I was young I thought money was the most important thing in life, now that I'm old — I know it is!

— Oscar Wilde

Your firm is a business. Put bluntly it is there to make money. It does this by selling the skills of its people and you are one of those people.

There are a number of consequences that flow from this simple truth.

- Your partners are interested in the returns from your work and not simply the intellectual exercise of doing it.

- You need to be aware of the commercial consequences of the projects you do and be able to talk about them.

  o Will the projects you are working on now (internal and external) make the firm a net return? What is the quantum of that return?

○ Do your projects contribute to the reputation of the firm? If so why is that important? Will it attract new clients? Will it allow the firm to charge more for this area of work in the future? Is it possible to put a quantum to the reputational contribution so that its value can be assessed?

○ Are your projects reducing costs? Will the profitability of work now or in the future be increased? Can the value be assessed?

○ Is your work ensuring the firm's long-term sustainability? Are you clear about how your work is doing this?

• The financial contribution you make to the firm will become more and more important to your promotion prospects as you move up the firm and will be vital to your partnership prospects when an explicit business case will need to be made around what you bring to the partnership.

Partners I talk to are often dismayed at what they see as the lack of commercial awareness of more junior staff and some suggest that there is a gender bias to this. The report Cracking The Code (KPMG, YSC and The 30% club, 2014, p. 14) suggested that in their development reviews 'applying commercial acumen' was seen as a strength in men and a weakness in women. Susan Colantuono also refers to this in her broader work with commercial organisations, suggesting that women are less inclined to explicitly consider the commercial and strategic business benefits of the work that they do (Colantuono, 2014).

I am a little uncomfortable about any perception that women are less commercially aware. I do not believe women's work is less commercially focussed, nor do I believe that women are less able to think and talk about the commercial benefits of the work they do. I do however find that when I get women to articulate what they offer the firm (see the exercise in Chapter 4) they talk initially about the inputs (working hard, technical knowledge) rather than the outputs (financial returns, cost reductions). It is only after they have been prompted to talk in more commercial terms that the full commercial value of their work is revealed.

I am not sure why women appear to need a prompt to talk more commercially; many certainly have a powerful commercial story to tell. I wonder if women are less exposed to the more commercial ad hoc conversations held outside the office in social situations because of their lack of sponsorship and therefore do not realise its importance. Alternatively, could it be that the continuation from academic life is stronger for women as it was those elements that drew them to professional service firms to start with? This could mean that the noncommercial aspects of working hard and becoming an expert are the elements they continue to focus on when asked to describe their work.

Whatever the cause of the perception, it is not difficult to address. You need to be clear about the financial contribution you make to your firm's business at all stages of your career.

There is usually somebody in your office or team who is responsible for pulling together the management accounts so that the partners know how the firm, office or business unit is doing. There will also be a business strategy for the firm, office or business unit. It is worth knowing who does this work and what part of it is available to you. It is a positive step to be interested and engaged with the commercial aspects of your firm and whilst professional service firms are notoriously secretive about their financial data you should make yourself aware of what is available to you.

WITHIN THIS STRATEGIC AND COMMERCIAL CONTEXT WHAT IS YOUR CONTRIBUTION?

Exercise
What do I contribute financially and in terms of business opportunities to the firm?

Review what you wrote in Chapter 4 about what you offer the firm and be clear about what this means in financial terms. What are the implications of what you offer in terms of cost reductions and revenue brought into the firm now and in the future?

What I offer the firm commercially:

•

●

●

How does this fit into the strategy of the firm or of your business unit?

WHAT ARE YOUR COMPETITORS UP TO?

You are in a competitive market as a firm. Do you know what your competitors are offering and how your firm is seen in the market compared with your major competitors? It is worth thinking about what you personally offer that adds to your firm's differentiated offering and articulating this.

BEING COMMERCIAL ABOUT YOUR CONTRIBUTION, YOUR VALUE AND YOUR PAY

Because of the hierarchical nature of professional service firms it is easy to assume that men and women at the same grade and the same performance level are paid equally. I know that Human Resources functions do a lot of work to ensure this is the case but there are anomalies. Anecdotal evidence suggests that men are much better at actively finding out what their market value is and communicating this within the firm. Women tend to rely on the system to pay them fairly.

This is an area where women can be branded as pushy, militant or strident so beware, but there is a way which sits between those unfair stereotypes of women arguing their cause and being a mouse who never raises the subject of her pay. Be prepared to find out the facts of what equivalent others are paid for equivalent work inside and outside the firm and if there are discrepancies calmly ask why.

MY CHALLENGES TO YOU

1. **Think** about and get interested in your firm as a business, particularly if your ambition is to be an owner of that business as a partner.

2. **Ask** for information – what is available to you about the current position and future strategic aspirations of the business unit you work within (whether that be your team, your department, your office or the firm).

3. **Talk** about what you offer in a way that shows you are aware of its commercial value and contribution.

Tips from the top — Advice from partners to women in their firm

'Know what you bring to the business'.

'You need to be very clear about what you do well and how you can make a difference'.

'You need to show that you can build a business, which is what the firm is about'.

'I need to be clear with myself and others about three things:

1. What is my business

2. What my role is in building that business

3. Why I am the person to be leading and building my business'.

RESOURCES

KPMG YSC and The 30% club. (2014). *Cracking the code*.

Colantuono, S. (2014). The career advice you probably didn't get. TED talk.

CHAPTER 16

DEVELOPING YOUR BUSINESS

*To be successful, you have to have your heart in
your business, and your business in your heart*
— Thomas Watson, former Chairman and
CEO of IBM

The first step in developing your business is to identify
what your business is. What is it that you offer your
clients? The women I work with know this, but many are
less clear when I drill down further. Why is your offer
different from your competitors? What is the potential
market for your type of services? What share of that
market do you currently have and what proportion of
that total do you think you should aim to have?

Women are good at building businesses, but there are
undoubtedly challenges that women face that men do not
encounter and many are unaware of. The good news is
that as a woman in a professional service firm you are
more likely to be remembered from any interaction as
you will stand out in a sea of grey suited men. The bad
news is that there are more client business development

events aimed at men; women tell me that male partners will often invite your male peers before thinking of you. There is also a subtle but important difference to consider in that if you take the initiative and invite male clients out yourself you need to ensure that this business invitation is not misconstrued as a social invitation.

WHY IS BUILDING RELATIONSHIPS WITH CLIENTS IMPORTANT?

At the core of successful business development is building trusting relationships with your clients and women are good at this. The following examples come from those buying legal services, but similar reactions come from clients buying other services from all professional service firms.

An interview with a senior in-house lawyer at an investment bank

We all work mostly over the phone and by Email in this business, but I think it is useful to get to know people personally and build up rapport with them, so it is great to get an invitation to an event or just to meet up for a coffee or a lunch. If external lawyers make the effort in this way it's much easier for us to call them with a query. When the next transaction comes up, I'll be thinking: they're great people at that firm and they've responded well to my questions — I will give them a try on this deal

— Hannah Langworth, Commercial Law Firms: the client perspective, article in the *Gateway* 2013

It is instructive to listen to clients when they articulate what they value about your service and their internal decision-making process. Many assumptions are made about what is important to clients. In the case of law firms the mismatch between what clients value and what firms think clients value has been articulated by Pennington Hennessy (2017) as follows:

Figure 16.1: What Clients Want.

What clients want	What law firms think their clients want
1. Affability — I want to work with people I like	1. Ability — I can fix your problem as I have the specialist expertise
2. Availability — I want to work with somebody who wants to work with me and can do	2. Availability — I can fix your problem now
3. Affordability — I want a transparent fee structure	3. Affability — let us concentrate on the matter in hand
4. Ability — since you work for a good firm I assume you are a good lawyer, so knowledge of my sector is more important to me than specialist expertise	4. Affordability — let us not talk money until after the meeting
Source: Adapted from Pennington, J. (2017, January 6). What do clients look for in a Lawyer?. Retrieved from http://www.penningtonhennessy.com/blog/what-do-clients-look-for-in-a-lawyer	

HOW TO BE YOUR CLIENT'S TRUSTED ADVISOR

I am often told that those working at all levels in a professional service firm are trying to be their client's trusted external advisor. This position of trusted advisor means that the firm is privy to the client's thought processes, meaning that it understands the client's needs now and in the future, putting the firm in a great position in any pitching processes. Whilst this aim is often talked about, what builds the trust in the relationship is less often articulated.

It is also true that those working with you within the firm also need to trust you, and you need to trust them, again it is worth thinking through what you can do to build trust and what are the elements that can destroy your trust in others and theirs in you.

THE TRUST EQUATION

Let us look at what is often referred to as the trust equation which separates what trust is made of:

$$T = \frac{C + R + I}{S}$$

T = Trust

C = Credibility. This is your qualifications and your reputation, individually and as part of the firm. The greater these are the more you will be trusted by the client. Be prepared to talk about what you bring to the job in terms of experience and qualifications; it will help the relationship and the work.

R = Reliability. This reflects whether you deliver on what you say you will do. The more you show you do what you promise the more you will be trusted by the client. Others talking about you might increase this but the main source is your client or your partner's experience of you.

I = Intimacy. A strange word to use in business but it is key. It reflects your interest in the client personally and their place in the organisation. The more you can make the client look good the more they will trust you; they need to feel that you would not let them down. Like reliability this is something that you prove over time and by reputation.

S = Self orientation. This reflects how clearly you are actually only interested in yourself. The higher this denominator is the less they will trust you.

HOW TO MAKE PRODUCTIVE RELATIONSHIPS WITH CLIENTS THAT WILL LEAD TO WORK

This could be a book in itself, but what I have learned from partners in professional service firms and the women and men that I have worked with can be summarised in these client relationship building tips.

- When engaging with your client you are not always expected to be in 'expert mode'. Asking questions of them about their work and their business shows that you are interested in them beyond getting work from them. In the trust equation this is reducing the denominator S.

- You do not need to be in 'sell mode' either. The best business developers I know think about their role as being able to help the client, facilitating the useful connections inside and outside the firm that the client needs. Of course you need to be able to talk about what you and the firm can do to help when it is appropriate, but the focus is not on what you want to sell but on what they need. If you are seen to be genuinely acting in their interests now they are more likely to come back to you. In the trust equation this is increasing the numerator I.

- Listen and learn about them, their lives and their business. I am often asked to come in to clients to teach men and women 'business awareness'. When I push to find out what they actually want, it is to know more about their client's businesses. Whilst there are things that you can pick up from reading a quality national newspaper's business section and their accounts, if you want to know more about your client's businesses my top tip is to be genuinely curious when you meet clients or potential clients — they are the experts in their businesses and the best people to learn from. I once worked with the General Counsel of a large global company in South Africa who explained that in the 6 months since she had taken on the role many firms had come and told her what they could do. Her complaint was that nobody had come and asked her what she wanted or listened when she tried to tell them. In the trust equation what she was requesting was increasing the numerator I and reducing the denominator S.

- Watching men play sports is not the only kind of client relationship building event possible. Ask clients out for breakfast or lunch. You need to eat these meals to keep your brain working so it is a win all round. It is a good idea to bring somebody else along from the firm and this facilitates helpful connections with other parts of the firm and ensures that there are no mixed messages about inviting a male client out for lunch if you have any concerns about this.

- Be prepared to talk to clients about work you are interested in or passionate about. In the trust equation this is increasing the numerator C.

- Always keep in touch with clients to ensure they never think you have over promised and under delivered; be interested in their feedback. In the trust equation this is increasing the numerator R.

- Don't ignore the clients at junior levels; everybody in the organisation has some influence and building relationships with clients is not just about engaging with the ultimate decision makers. The people you interact with now may well be the decision makers of the future in this or other organisations; engage and make links with them.

CLIENT RELATIONSHIP BUILDING EVENTS

I have often been told that it is harder for women to get invited to business development events as they often involve watching men playing sport and the assumption is that women will not be interested. There are, of course, alternative relationship building events at theatres, art galleries and concert halls. If appropriate, you might want to consider making those that are organising the event aware that you would like to come even if it is to watch a football or rugby match, or that they might want to consider an alternative event to include the women at the client and within the firm.

Many women, some in frustration at not being invited to 'male orientated' relationship building events, use women's business networks very effectively to make contacts with clients or potential clients. It is worth looking at what your firm does in this area or what is going on in your locality.

CROSS SELLING WORK

Cross selling your firm's services is important for the commercial survival of the firm and for your success in it. 'Warm' leads from others within your firm are a really easy way to make connections and be considered for work and if you make leads for others in the firm from your clients they will often reciprocate.

My question here is 'what do you know about what your firm does other than in your specialism?'. Might it be worth going to lunch with your colleagues who work in other parts of the firm? You could ask them about what they do, what they could offer your clients and you could tell them about what you do. Whatever your level, a network within the firm is a useful source of information and a means of ensuring others have the right impression of you (see Chapter 11).

HUNTING AND FARMING

There is a lot of emphasis on bringing in new business in professional service firms. A stereotype that I often hear is that men are good at being hunters (meaning that they go out and find new work from new clients) and women are good at being farmers (developing work from existing clients). The complaint from women is that the hunting is lauded as if it were more valuable than the farming. I am not sure whether it really is seen to be more valuable if work is won from new clients or that men are better at talking about what they do and therefore it is better known and valued.

My tip is to talk about the additional work you have won wherever it comes from. Take ownership of these successes. Even if you think they have come easily to you that does not mean they would have come to others. The people who make decisions about your career need to know what you are achieving for their firm wherever it comes from.

WHO CAN HELP YOU?

If your firm has business development specialists it is worth going to talk to them to learn about what they do and how they can help you. It is also worth getting any juniors who work with you involved in researching possible clients that might be interested in your services. This is useful for their development as it helps them see the firm as a business and the importance of gaining more work.

QUESTIONS TO REFLECT ON

Exercise
Questions you might find useful:

The strategy

- Have you asked for the business strategy for the team?
- Have you considered what areas of this strategy you could get involved with?

Your contacts

- Are your contacts on the firm's client database?

- Do you take the time to update the firm's client database to let partners know of the client contacts that you have?

- Do you keep in contact with people you work with at the client after the specific piece of work finishes?

What can you learn from others?

- Do you see others developing business? If so how do they do it?

- How do people at your level use their networks for creating business opportunities?

- What are the examples you see around you, both within the firm and outside it, of how other women develop their businesses successfully?

- What could you do to learn from the men and women you know who have developed successful businesses?

- What support do you need to help you with this?

Your competitors

- What are your competitors offering?

- How does this compare with what you offer?

MY CHALLENGES TO YOU

1. Be more interested in your clients and not just the current task you are doing for them. What are their

challenges and who do you know that could help them? *Ask one open question at each client meeting in the next month to learn more about them.*

2. Think about who else could benefit from the work you do. How could you engage with them and how could you help them? Find out who else in the firm is interested in them and who else knows them. *Put some time in your diary now to think about this, collect information and make a plan. Then execute the plan.*

3. Find out what other people in the firm do that could help you, your existing clients and potential clients. This is important but not urgent, so will need a planned approach, but it could be fun. *Make the plan, then do it.*

Tips from the top — Advice from partners to women in their firm

'You need to develop your clients' trust which is something that women are good at'.

'Work out who you have rapport with at the client and talk to them. Rapport is important'.

'Be interested in your client as a person and in their business'.

'Make your client contact look good'.

'I am still in contact with the clients I knew when I was a junior. We have developed together and now they are senior decision makers who trust me'.

'Little but often is how I keep contact with my clients and targets'.

'Ensure others in the firm know what you do and what you are passionate about'.

'If female networking can help you make useful contacts and develop work — do it'.

'Team up with others to do your business development — it is more fun'.

'You need to be innovative in the service you give. You can develop business in different ways'.

'I took time and effort to understand what else the firm did — it was important'.

'It is terribly important to listen to the client and not just operate from your own specialism'.

'Keep your head up and look for new opportunities'.

RESOURCES

Maister, D. (2005). Do you really want relationships? Retrieved from http://davidmaister.com/articles/do-you-really-want-relationships/

Green, C. H., & Andrea, P. (2011). *Howe, Trusted advisor fieldbook*. John Wiley & Sons.

CHAPTER 17

MAKING THE MOST OF YOUR APPRAISALS

It is not in the stars to hold our destiny but in ourselves.

— William Shakespeare

This is a key interaction for your career and the good news is that you don't need to ask for it; in most cases the firm sets it up for you. This does not mean that you do not need to prepare carefully for it. If you do not take your career seriously in this golden opportunity then you are sending out a clear message to the firm that you are not that serious about your career.

BEING PROACTIVE RATHER THAN REACTIVE

I heard from one very successful partner that before making partner what he did at the start of every year was to review the appraisal document that would be used at the end of the year so that he was clear what the firm wanted from him. He then planned his work during the year to ensure that he could show work under all of the sections and detailed criteria set out in the appraisal document. It is a strategy that worked very well for him as he reached his goal of partnership at a very young age. The appraisal documents are there to reflect what the firm wants from you and using them as a proactive tool rather than a reactive form makes a lot of sense.

Even if you do not use the form proactively, waiting until the end of the year to think about what you have done during the year is not a great strategy; it means that you are not taking control of the experience you are getting and where it is leading you. It would be more helpful for your career if you kept a running draft of your appraisal document during the year. This means that you are aware of where the gaps are when you still have time to fill them and you do not forget the excellent things you did in April when the appraisal comes around in the following March.

Get feedback during the year when it is fresh in everybody's mind so that you have the information early enough to capitalise on your strengths and mitigate your weaknesses during the year (see Chapter 6). It is important as a woman that you ask for specific feedback about the areas you are interested in (see Chapter 6 for help in this) as there is evidence to suggest that women get much more generic feedback which is less useful. Ask for examples and what you could do differently.

HOW WOMEN TALK ABOUT THEIR ACHIEVEMENTS

There is considerable evidence that men and women tend to attribute their successes and their failures differently.

Men tend to attribute their successes to their own hard work and expertise and their failures to external factors such as an impossible task, bad luck and a troublesome team. Women tend to do the opposite, attributing success externally to an easy task, good luck and a great team, whilst they internalise their failures taking on personal responsibility and not acknowledging the external factors. Neither tendency is balanced and helpful. It is worth being consciously aware of these tendencies so that you can review what you say about how the year has gone and strive to have a more balanced view of what has contributed to what you have (and have not) achieved.

THE APPRAISAL CONVERSATION

Ideally appraisal conversations are held separately from development conversations as the former looks backwards and the latter concentrates on the future. Appraisal conversations are often used to determine pay and are for a different purpose to the development conversations where you might wish to be more honest about your weaknesses. However, as the same two people are involved (you and your appraising partner) firms usually combine these discussions.

Thus there are broadly four elements in an appraisal/ development conversation:

Looking backwards:

1. What went well and learning points

2. What did not go well and learning points

Looking forwards:

3. Targets for next year

4. Long-term career plans

My experience has been that in general men and women approach these conversations differently. A tendency for women to aim for perfection and a nervousness about bragging, which is less socially acceptable in women, can lead to a difference in the focus of the conversation. Men tend to concentrate on items 1 and 4 above and women often focus their time and attention on items 2 and 3. Neither of these approaches is ideal as all four areas need to be covered.

If you follow the more typical female pattern it has two consequences:

- You leave it up to the reviewer to bring in all your strengths and if the reviewer is not skilled enough to do this well, or does not have the appropriate information the conversation can be either rather anodyne or negative in tone.

- You do not leave enough time to talk about your long-term plans so that the reviewer is free to make assumptions about what you are interested in and how ambitious you are. As we saw in Chapter 5 if you do not state clearly what your ambitious are some will assume that as a woman, or particularly as a woman who might or does have children, your ambitions are limited. Indeed if you do not talk about your long-term career plans at all, the assumption may be that you do not care about them or do not have them.

HOW TO PREPARE FOR YOUR ANNUAL APPRAISAL DISCUSSIONS

The most important point is to put sufficient time aside in your diary to prepare. Do not leave it until all your client work is done and start preparing for it late at night. Do the preparation when your brain is at its best in the morning and you have enough time to draft and review what you want to say. Perhaps the meeting with MS in the month before your appraisal meeting is a good time to start the preparation (see Chapter 3). This time needs protecting — it is important.

Exercise

Think holistically first — what do you want to get out of the conversation? What do you want the appraiser to think about you, to feel about you and what do you want them to do as a result of the conversation?

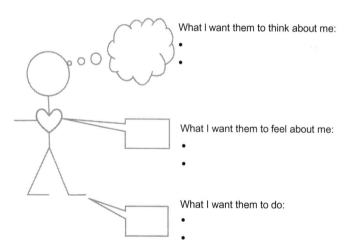

What I want them to think about me:
-
-

What I want them to feel about me:
-
-

What I want them to do:
-
-

With that as the backdrop start preparing for each part of the meeting. Ensure you have enough time to focus on item 4, long-term career plans. My advice would be to prepare in the order 4–1 so that everything is set in the context of where you want to be going.

Much of what we have covered in this book will be relevant to this preparation. In particular:

- What you offer the firm (Chapter 4)

- Your ambitions (Chapter 5)

- The feedback you have received (Chapter 6)

- Your strengths, weaknesses, opportunities and threats (Chapter 7)

- What you want others to say about you (Chapter 8)

- Stepping forward (Chapter 10)

- Being commercial (Chapter 15)

Exercise
What do I want to communicate at my appraisal

1. What went well this year:	Learning points:
a. My part	
b. External factors	

2. What did not go well this year:	Learning points:
a. My part	
b. External factors	
3. Targets for next year:	Support and challenge needed:
4. Long-term career objectives:	Support and challenge needed:

Once you have prepared, allow the appraiser to prepare. Consider sending them a draft agenda before the review so that they have time to think. The agenda may simply be the four headings or you might want to include more information, think about what you know of your appraiser and what will be the most effective format for the two of you. The key thing is to give them time to think, this may be the first time they have heard you ask about long-term opportunities and it would be useful to you if they come to the meeting prepared.

In the meeting make it clear that you want to talk about all four elements and agree how you are going to divide the time.

After the meeting follow up as you would with any other important meeting. Write up the notes and corresponding actions for both you and the appraiser with deadlines and check-in points as appropriate.

THE RELATIONSHIP BETWEEN YOU AND YOUR FIRM

There is often an implicit, reciprocal 'development contract' between you and your firm and it is worth explicitly considering it in preparation for your appraisal. There are things the firm provides for you and in turn it expects from you. Are you clear about what you need from your firm and what your responsibilities are? For example:

Your firm may provide:

- The framework (training and development programmes, performance review and assessment systems, grade structure and promotion criteria).

- The experience (the client base, opportunities to work in different areas of the firm, a variety of internal management roles and different services to clients).

- Advice (from partners, staff and HR).

- The feedback so that you know where you are and where you are heading.

In return do you provide:

- the intellectual ability, optimism, proactivity, will and energy to make what you want from your career?

- the motivation, initiative and determination to look for opportunities to do your best?

- the flexibility to turn your hand to many different tasks and roles?

- the input (you need to tell the firm what you want so that they can help you get it)?

- the maturity to be reasonable about linking your career plans to the firm's needs?

MY CHALLENGES FOR YOU

1. Start thinking proactively about how you are doing now — *draft your appraisal now (at your next MS meeting? — see Chapter 3) and update it on a regular basis.*

2. Be active in your appraisal discussions — *start by planning and setting an agenda so that you are getting what you need from the discussions as well as giving the appraising partner the information you want them to have.*

Tips from the top — Advice from partners to women in their firm

'Ask for what you need'.

'You need to be very clear about what you bring to the mix'.

'If clients are saying how good you are take advantage of this'.

'Different styles are OK, the firm needs them'.

RESOURCES

Cuddy, A. Your body language shapes who you are.
TED talk.

Kay, K., & Shipman, C. (2014). The confidence gap.
The Atlantic Magazine.

Saujani, R. Teach girls bravery not perfection. TED talk.

CHAPTER 18

PREPARING FOR PROMOTION PROCESSES

This is where the elements brought together in the last 17 chapters bear fruit. You are known for the good things that you do and it is known that you are interested in promotion, you have a sponsor who is actively working for you, helping you navigate the politics and making the introductions necessary. Your developmental plan has succeeded; now you are being considered for promotion.

If you are not being prepared for promotion now, but might be in the future you still need to skim read this chapter to prepare yourself in good time. Promotion processes are by definition testing and to ensure your experience is both successful and as comfortable as possible you need to be aware and prepare. My experience has been that women feel this preparation is more important than their male peers, so give yourself what you need in terms of time to prepare.

I have focussed on what is the most onerous promotion process, that for partner, as it is the most comprehensive.

If that is not the promotion you are working towards now you can ignore the elements that are partner specific.

WHAT IS THE PROCESS? WHAT IS NEEDED, FROM WHOM AND BY WHEN?

I have coached many women (and men) in many different professional service firms during their promotion to partner and my first piece of advice in every case is to find out all you can about the promotion process you are about to embark on. This sounds obvious, but often promotion processes in professional service firms are incredibly opaque and accurate information is hard to find. The more time you give yourself for this information to come to light the better.

It is worth mentioning that there are often two consecutive 'processes' which you have to pass to become a partner. The first is the informal 'process' to get the support of the partners in your team so that you can enter the second official partnership selection process. The first selection process will vary from team to team and you will need to use your network to determine how to navigate it as it may not be written down or formalised in any way. The official process is usually run by HR in conjunction with senior partners and there is likely to be a formal methodology to this process.

My experience is that that whilst there is secrecy about levels of remuneration in partnerships, the partners themselves are unaware that others are not informed about the promotion processes and are very happy to share their understanding. This openness is laudable, but not always very helpful as it can mean that there are several historic versions of the process and what is needed circulating. My advice would be to ask for the current formal process set out in writing from your HR contact and if this is not available talk to a number of sources to get all the information you can.

The most useful sources of information are:

- HR

- The firm's intranet

- Your sponsor, appraising partner or supporters, particularly if they have sponsored a candidate through the process recently

- Those in your network who have been through the process recently

It is important that you can fill in the table on the following pages with information or have a clear, unequivocal understanding that this is not relevant to you.

MOBILISING YOUR SUPPORT

As you prepare for the promotion process you need to work simultaneously on two strands of work: the excellent day job you do and the promotion process that you are involved with.

This is the time to ask for help. It is not a sign of weakness, it is a strategic imperative to ensure you can show the firm what you are capable of. So often in professional service firms candidates are silent about the fact that they are going through the promotion processes as if it is a

What needs doing?	What is the deadline?	Who is responsible?	What can you do?
The business case that supports my promotion — why should the firm promote somebody?			Find out who will compile this case Contribute to this case: • Think commercially about what you do: ○ The size of your market ○ The potential growth ○ The position of competitors • Think about how the firm is going to make more money by giving you a promotion.
The personal case for my promotion — why am I the perfect candidate for this slot?			Formulate this case: Look at your feedback and articulate your strengths clearly and concisely. See Chapters 4, 6 and 8.
Help others to understand what you currently do and what you could contribute to the firm in the future			Help your sponsor and supporters by giving them the information they need to talk about the business case and what you bring. See Chapter 12 which sets out what your sponsor's role is and what they will need.

Formal paperwork		Know what it covers and when it is due. Plan your communications so that the appropriate information has been given to the appropriate people by that date. See below for advice
Interviews		Know what they are testing, how many people will be involved, their roles, what the format will be and what will be required of you. See below for advice
Assessment events		Know what they are testing, how many people will be involved, their roles, what the format will be and what will be required of you. See below for advice
The business as usual 'day job'		Mobilise your support so that you are not overloaded. Plan Delegate See below for advice

guilty secret, or the worst thing in the world to fail if people know about it. Unsurprisingly most people around you will know what is happening; professional service firms are not good at keeping those kind of internal secrets, but because you are being secretive others are not able to offer help.

Allow those who are around you and care about you to make their contribution. It may come from those at home, it is also likely to come from those around you at work. For example, the junior that works for you may be delighted that you are up for promotion. The likelihood is that they are part of your team and a promotion in the team is usually seen as a welcome sign that the team is renewing itself and growing. It may also show that those around you have more of a chance to step into your shoes and get promotion themselves. Think about asking them for help in the next few months. You may need them to step up and do more of the 'day job'. This is good for you and for them as well as being good preparation for the new status quo when you achieve promotion. One of the questions partners are interested in when considering a candidate for promotion is who will do your role as you move up. This is an ideal time to allow those who sit below you to show what they are capable of.

The other source of support you need at this point is from your sponsor. Their role is vital and I have seen excellent candidates struggle because their sponsor failed to do their job. This is rare as the sponsor is very exposed if they do not get you through; they are risking their reputation on you. Review Chapter 12 on sponsorship to be clear about what your sponsor should be doing for you and make suggestions if you feel there is more that they could do.

Your clients will often be interested in you and your progression. Depending on your relationship and the culture within their organisation this may be a really good time to ask them for feedback, particularly on what you do well. You could tell them you are up for promotion and ask them for feedback. If you have been doing a good job this request usually elicits useful feedback that reflects how you are seen externally and client feedback is given a lot of weight.

PREPARING THE PAPERWORK

There is usually a lot of paperwork which supports your business and personal case for promotion.

The paperwork may not be prepared by you, but I strongly suggest that you ask to give input. This allows you to remind those around you of any excellent things that you do that are not already reflected. It also allows you to feel comfortable in any interviews or assessment events that will refer back to your paperwork.

If you are asked to prepare the paperwork, ensure you are given a template or ask for a redacted version of the paperwork submitted successfully by somebody in your network so that you know how you should structure your case. Ask for advice, this is not a sign of weakness but a strategic strength, showing the network that will be essential to you in the new role.

Do not look at your paperwork last thing at night after you have done all your other work. It is really important and if you do not give it the attention or importance that your career deserves then others will follow your lead.

Review what has been written:

- Your promotion is a commercial decision by the firm. Ensure that you put in the relevant numbers to reflect your case.

- Link the non-client facing activities you do to their commercial benefits. Think of the things that you do that are vital but unseen — the 'organisational dusting'. For example, staff training is a way of ensuring the firm is sustainable and maximises profits; not a kindness to the juniors.

- Think about how newspapers get your attention; ensure that the most important facts are at the top of any section.

- Think about the order of your points and ensure they reflect what is likely to be the reader's order of importance.

- Watch out for words that undermine your case. If you are leading a team say so and don't say that you are managing or coordinating them. Don't use words like 'just', 'quite' or 'a bit'.

Once you are happy with your paperwork get somebody who knows what you do to review it. This does not have to be limited to those at work; often people at home are useful reviewers as they have heard you talk about work and will remember key points that you might have forgotten about.

Get your sponsor and supporters (see Chapter 12) to review your paperwork. Your sponsor needs to be completely happy with it to do their job. Your supporters may wish to contribute to the case, but also need to know what is being said as you also want them to be out there talking about you and your case in an informed way.

ASSESSMENTS

Whatever assessment method is used my suggestion is that you prepare fully and practice where possible.

Top Tips for Interviews

There are often interviews associated with important promotions. You want the interviewers to see what you are capable of and so it is important that you prepare carefully.

Before the Day
- Do your research on the interview panel members. What are their backgrounds and interests? Use your network to find out what you can about them.

- Do your research on the structure of the panel, the requirements and any favourite questions from others who have been through interview panels recently.

- Arrange a practice interview panel with your sponsor or supporters. Make it as real as you can; answering questions in your head is different from doing it for real.

- Get to see the room before the day of the interview (if possible) so that there are no surprises.

- Plan what you are going to wear (something you feel comfortable and great in) and try it on a week before-hand to ensure you are happy with it.

- Think about your weaknesses and how you are work-ing on them so that you can be honest but leave others with the impression that you are aware and proactive about your development.

- Think about five situations in which you did brilliantly and showed off your skills. These will need to be front of mind in the interview — see below for the STAR for-mat that the panel may use.

- Get a decent night's sleep. If you have small children consider using a hotel or an agreement with your part-ner that they deal with any crises in the night before and the day of the interview.

On the Day

- Don't take calls in the couple of hours before the inter-view. You cannot control what they are about and they can undermine or destabilise you.

- Do set up a call with somebody who makes you feel fabulous before you go in. Not to share how nervous you are but to be told how brilliant you are.

- Amy Cuddy is an associate professor at Harvard Business School. She has done some interesting work on what happens to our hormones when we sit or stand in a high or low power pose. Her suggestion is that before going into any interview you stand for two minutes in a high power pose to boost your testosterone (a hormone that gives you confidence) and quell your cortisol (the stress hormone). Her conclusion was that this small act and the resultant hormonal changes can positively contribute to interview results in a statistically significant way. I know some that I have worked with found this useful, but I would suggest that if you try it out you do your power pose in private! (A. Cuddy. Your body language shapes who you are. TED talk).

In the Interview

- Go in to the room as an adult. You are not a child in the teacher's staff room, rather you are a skilled professional who is here to show how good you are.

- Remember they want you to succeed and you simply need to give them the information to allow them to tick boxes (and in the case of partnership to see you as a credible peer).

- Give yourself time if your mind becomes blank:
  - Breathe
  - Buy time by simple phrases like 'that is an interesting question'/'let me think'
  - Take the time to give yourself a sip of water to give your brain time to move from the limbic system of fight or flight to the neocortex where language and logic reside

- If you do not think you answered something well you can always say 'I don't think I gave you what I wanted to say there, the key points are...'.

- Be commercial — this is about your contribution to the firm as a business.

- They may be using the STAR model of questioning:

  o Give me a Situation where you showed X (leadership/ability to deal with a difficult situation, etc.). This is fair as it allows you to choose the situation you want to talk about.

  o What was your Task — what were you trying to achieve?

  o What was your Action — what did YOU actually do?

  o What was the Result? This should include your learning.

It is worth thinking through a handful of situations which you would like to talk about in this format so that you can bring them easily to mind in the interview.

Appendix 1 gives you some of the questions; those that I have worked with have told me that they have been asked. This may be helpful to review as part of your preparation.

Top Tips for Assessment Events

These take many forms and it is vital you know what the format is. Many include interviews, case studies and group discussions. Ensure you have the most recent format from HR or whoever is running the event.

The tips given above for interviews apply equally to many of these elements.

ADDITIONAL TIPS FOR GROUP DISCUSSIONS

- Some find it useful to say something early on to enter the conversation. Even 'that makes sense' or 'I agree' marks your place at the table, allowing you to join in more easily.

- Be aware of your body language; it too contributes to how you are perceived and the contribution you make.

- Part of what they are looking for is your ability to work with others, so it is important that you contribute fully but don't take over.

- Listen carefully to what others are saying; it is not a competition and their contributions can be very helpful to you and the task.

ADDITIONAL TIPS FOR CASE STUDIES

- Case studies are there to see how you tackle an issue and rarely have a 'right answer'.

- Those assessing you are interested in how you work on it and who you would involve.

- Be commercial, risk aware and think widely about both the situation and those involved. There is usually both a task and a human element to the tricky case and you need to address both.

- It is the quality of your mind that they are primarily interested in so be prepared to articulate your thought processes.

MY CHALLENGES TO YOU

1. *Prepare.* Read this chapter carefully before you are in the promotion process so that you can be prepared by gathering and giving information in good time. This makes the whole thing much less stressful.

2. *Get support and advice.* Use your network for feedback, help and support.

3. *Be authentic.* Do not try to be anybody else. If you get through on the basis of being inauthentic you will probably be found out and if you do get through the process then you may not be ready to do the job.

Tips from the top — Advice from partners to women in their firm

'Get hold of other people's businesses cases — they are really useful'.

'Get the team behind you and to support you. You need them'.

'Assess what you are going to do against what you need to show on your business case. If you have already shown you can do something, it may be time to allow another to do it'.

'You need to understand the promotion process and use your network to prepare'.

'I love my job. Being a partner is the best job I have ever had'.

'New partnership can be a lonely place; you feel even more responsible. You need to find the right group of people to support you'.

'It is difficult to make decisions initially as a partner, but as you do this more and more the confidence grows. The weight of responsibility feels higher when you first become a partner, and therefore your confidence will dip, but this will be reversed in time'.

'I had to find my personal answer to the question 'why do I want to be a partner?'.

'I found it really useful to have a peer group of new partners that I could bounce ideas off'.

RESOURCE

Cuddy, A. Your body language shapes who you are. TED talk.

APPENDIX

QUESTIONS FROM PROMOTION PANELS

The following are questions coachees reported that they were asked in promotion panels in professional service firms. Not all will be relevant to you and your promotion, and your colleagues who have been through promotion panels recently are an excellent source of advice and examples.

The 'can you give me an example of a situation where you ...' questions are scattered through the following list and are often used as part of the STAR questioning technique. I have marked them with *. The interviewers ask you this opening question below as a starter before pursuing the following line of questioning:

- Situation — can you give me an example of a situation where you ....

- Task — what were you trying to achieve ...

- Actions — what did you do ...

- Results — what were the outcomes ...

More guidance on preparing for such questions is given in Chapter 18.

EXAMPLE QUESTIONS

The following questions are a useful additional source to widen your thinking during your preparation alongside Chapter 18.

This promotion

1. Why do you want this role?

2. What difference will it make to the firm if you have this promotion?

3. As you step up into this role who will take on the tasks you have been doing in your current role?

4. What do you think you will find hardest about doing this role?

5. What are the biggest risks to your success in your new role?

What you do and how you do it?

6. What are you most proud of at work?

7. Can you give us an example of innovative action that you have taken?*

8. Can you give an example of an unexpected change on a client project (e.g., team, deliverables, objectives, timeline) and how you dealt with it?*

9. Can you give us an example of a project where you performed well/badly?*

10. Can you give us an example of how you flex your leadership style depending on the situation?*

11. Can you give us an example of how you flex your communication style?*

12. What are your strengths?

13. What are your weaknesses?

14. What is your role in relation to risk management? How will this change with promotion?

Your reaction to challenges

15. What is the most difficult thing you have to deal with on a day to day basis?*

16. What has been your biggest challenge with regard to managing staff?*

17. What is the most difficult thing you have had to deal with in the past?*

18. What is the biggest mistake you have ever made at work?*

19. What is the biggest mistake that someone working for you has made — what did you do?*

Influence and interaction with others

20. Can you give me an example of you influencing a client's decision making?*

21. What has been your biggest challenge with regard to managing staff?*

22. Who are your most important stakeholders and why?

23. Can you give us a situation where you have had to bring someone round to your way of thinking?*

24. Can you give us an example of a disagreement you had with a colleague at work?*

25. Can you give us an example of a situation where you had to stand up to peer pressure/to disagree with someone more senior than yourself at work?*

26. Tell me about a time when you have had to give difficult feedback — to a junior, to a senior, to a peer?*

27. Can you give us an example of how you coach junior staff on the job?*

28. Tell us about a time when you have acted to resolve conflict in your team.*

29. Can you talk to us about a time when you have made a poor decision at work, and how did it impact your team?*

The firm

30. What are the biggest challenges facing the firm?

31. If you were the senior partner of this firm/office/service line what would you worry about?

32. How do you assess the firm's competitors?

33. If someone asked you why should they use this firm, what would you tell them?

Your own development

34. What kind of leader do you aspire to be?

35. Can you give us an example of where you have been successful in developing yourself?*

36. What is the most insightful feedback you have ever been given?

37. Tell me about a time when you received difficult feedback?*

38. How do you manage you work/life balance? How will this job affect that?

39. How have you worked on your weaknesses?

Your clients

40. What are your clients worried about?

41. Why do your clients come to the firm?

42. What do we offer your clients that others do not?

43. What is the major threat to our work with your clients?

44. What are the biggest opportunities for new growth for your team in the next year?

45. What is your most important client relationship, why?

WIDER RESOURCES

There are lots of brilliant resources that can help you. My favourites are the short video talks and articles (ironic as I have just written a book) but they give you a taster and allow you to follow the links through to the book if you want to know more.

VIDEO TALKS

Brown, B. The power of vulnerability. TED talk.

Colantuono, S. The career advice you probably didn't get. TED talk.

Cuddy, A. Your body language shapes who you are. TED talk.

Heffernan, M. Wilful blindness and dare to disagree. TED talk.

Mohr, T. Playing big and inner critic. TED talks.

Pink, D. Drive: the surprising truth about what motivates us. RSA animation.

Reid, E. Why we pretend to be workaholics. *HBR Ideacast.*

Sandberg, S. Why we have too few women leaders. TED talk.

Saujani, R. Teach girls bravery not perfection. TED talk.

Shirley, D. S. Why do ambitious women have flat heads. TED talk.

Slaughter, A. M. Can we have it all? TED talk.

Tomasdottir, H. Feminine response to Iceland's financial crisis. TED talk.

ARTICLES SPECIFICALLY ABOUT WOMEN IN PROFESSIONAL SERVICE FIRMS

Kumra, S., & Vinnicombe, S. (2008). A study of the promotion to partner process in a professional services firm: How women are disadvantaged. *British Journal of Management,* 19, s65–s74.

The road less travelled; why women's path to partnership in consulting firms is still not straight. *NBI Consulting and Source 2015.*

USEFUL RESEARCH STUDIES WITH PARTICULAR RELEVANCE TO PROFESSIONAL SERVICE FIRMS

The McKinsey Women Matter series of articles and research studies.

PwC, *The Female Millennial: A new era of talent* 2015.

Cracking the code — KPMG YSC and The 30% club 2014 — UK sample.

KPMG Women's Leadership Study — Moving Women Forward into Leadership Roles — US sample, 2016.

ARTICLES

Correll, S., & Simard, C. (2016). Vague feedback is holding women back. *Harvard Business Review*, April 29.

Eagly, A., & Carli, L. (2007). Women and the labyrinth of leadership. *Harvard Business Review*.

James, K. T., & Arroba, T. (2005). Reading and Carrying. *Management Learning*.

Kay, K., & Shipman, C. (2014). The confidence gap. *The Atlantic Magazine*, May.

Knight, R. (2016). How to fake it when you are not feeling confident. *Harvard Business Review*, June.

Molinsky, A. (2016). Everybody suffers from imposter syndrome — here's how to handle it. *Harvard Business Review*, June.

Schwartz, T., & McCarthy, C. (2007). Manage your energy not your time. *Harvard Business Review*, October.

van Ogtrop, K. (2015). Why ambition is not working for women. *Time Magazine*, October 12.

BOOKS

Babcock, L., & Laschever, S. (2008). *Why women don't ask: The high cost of avoiding negotiation – and positive strategies for change.* Upper Saddle River, NJ: Princeton University Press.

Babcock, L., & Laschever, S. (2009). *Ask for it: How women can use the power of negotiation to get what they really want.* New York, NY: Bantam Dell.

Barsh, J., & Cranston, S. (2012). *How remarkable women lead: The breakthrough model for work and life.* New York, NY: Crown Business.

Bohnet, I. (2016). *What works: Gender equality by design.* Cambridge, MA: The Belknap Press of Harvard University Press.

Cain, S. (2013). *Quiet: The power of introverts in a world that can't stop talking.* London: Penguin Books.

Cuddy, A. (2016). *Presence: Bringing your boldest self to your biggest challenges.* London: Orion Publishing Group Ltd.

Gladwell, M. (2002). *The tipping point: How little things can make a big difference.* USA: Little, Brown and Company.

Goleman, D. (2014). *Focus: The hidden driver of excellence.* New York, NY: HarperCollins Publishers.

Goleman, D. (1999). *Working with Emotional intelligence.* Bloomsbury Publishing PLC.

Grant, A. (2016). *Originals: How Non-conformists change the world.* London: Ebury Publishing.

HBR: *10 best reads − leadership/managing yourself/managing others,* Harvard Business School Press. This series of volumes pull together what the editors of the Harvard Business Review consider to be the best HBR articles in a given business subject area.

Heffernan, M. (2012). *Wilful blindness: Why we ignore the obvious.* London: Simon & Schuster UK Ltd.

Hewlett, S.A. (2013). *Forget a mentor, find a sponsor: The new way to fast-track your career.* Boston, MA: Harvard Business Review Press.

Hewlett, S.A. (2014). *Executive presence: The missing link between merit and success.* New York, NY: HarperCollins Publishers.

Huffington, A. (2015). *Thrive: The third metric to redefining success and creating a happier life.* London: WH Allen.

Ibarra, H. (2015). *Act like a leader, think like a leader.* Boston, MA: Harvard Business Review Press.

Kay, K., & Shipman, C. (2015). *The confidence code: The science and art of self-assurance − what women should know.* New York, NY: HarperCollins Publishers.

Meers, S., & Strober, J. (2013). *Getting to 50/50, how working parents can have it all.* Piatus.

Mohr, T. (2015). *Playing big: A practical guide for brilliant women like you.* London: Penguin Random House.

Rock, D. (2009). *Your brain at work.* HarperBusiness.

Sandberg, S. (2013). *Lean in: Women, work, and the will to lead*. London: WH Allen.

Shipman, C., & Kay, K. (2009). *Womenomics: Work less, achieve more, live better*. New York, NY: HarperCollins Publishers.

Slaughter, A-M. (2015). *Unfinished business: Women men work family*. Canada: Random House Trade Paperbacks.

Tannen, D. (1996). *Talking From 9-5: Women and men at work: language, sex and power*. New York: HarperCollins Publishers Inc.

Thomson, P., Laurent, C., & Lloyd, T. (2015). *The rise of the female executive: How women's leadership is accelerating cultural change*. Hampshire: Palgrave Macmillan.

Williams, J. C., & Dempsey, R. (2014). *What works for women at work: Four patterns working women need to know*. New York & London: New York University Press.

Wittenberg-Cox, A. (2010). *How women mean business: A step by step guide to profiting from gender balanced business*. West Sussex: John Wiley & Sons Ltd.

Wittenberg-Cox, A., & Maitland, A. (2009). *Why Women Mean Business*, West Sussex: John Wiley & Sons Ltd.

ABOUT THE AUTHOR

Alison Temperley leads the design, delivery and coaching of global women's leadership programmes for Linklaters and Allen & Overy, and co-leads the global programme for Bird & Bird. She was also the coaching designer and joint programme director for the EY EMEIA women's leadership programme for 8 years, working with Cranfield University.

Alison has worked both for and with professional service firms for over 30 years. A qualified Chartered Accountant, with a master's degree in Organisational Psychodynamics, she combines practical business experience with an understanding of the driving forces that shape the careers of those who work for partnerships. Her business experience ranges from senior client-facing roles to the Head of Career Development for PwC's EMEA tax and legal practice.

INDEX

Alliances, 97, 100, 102, 103

Ambition, 45

    advice from partners to women in their firm, 61

    ambition at work, 52

    career management, 45–46

    communication mismatch, 53–55

    expressing, 56–58

    my challenges to you, 60–61

    timing of expressing, 59–60

    what do you want, 47–49

        work/life balance, 46

    your choice, 55

Anonymous feedback, 65–66

Appraisal(s)

    advice from partners to women in their firm, 191

    annual appraisal preparation, 187–190

    being proactive rather than reactive, 183–184

    conversation, 185–186

    development 'contract', 190–191

    my challenges to you, 191

    talking about your achievements, 184–185

Appraisal preparation, 187–190

Assessments for promotion processes, 201

    assessment events tips, 204

    interviews tips, 201–204

Attributable feedback, 66–67

    simple model for, 67–68

Authenticity, 11

Brief, Enthusiastic, Successful, Take-aways (BEST), 88–89

    response, 126

Building relationships with clients, 172–173

Bull (or elephant) in china shop, politics, 99

Business, 163, 171

Business development, 171

    advice from partners to women in their firm, 181–182

    business development specialists, 179

    building relationships with clients, 172–173

    client relationship building events, 177–178

client's trusted advisor,
173–174
cross selling work, 178
hunting and farming,
178–179
interview with senior in-
house lawyer, 172
my challenges to you,
180–181
productive relationships
with clients,
175–177
professionals in firm, 125
questions, 179–180
trust equation, 174–175

Career, 9
advice from partners to
women in their
firm, 14
authenticity, 11
development, 18–19
learning cycle, 12–13
management, 27
my challenges to you,
13–14
what do you want, 10–11
Clever foxes, politics, 99
Client relationship building
events, 177–178
Clients, productive
relationships with,
175–177
Client's trusted advisor,
173–174
Clients important, building
relationships with,
172–173
Commercial
advice from partners to
women in their
firm, 169

benefits, 165
commercial about
contribution, value
and pay, 167–168
competitors, 167
consequences, 163
financial contribution, 164
my challenges to you,
168–169
strategic and commercial
context, 166–167
Communication mismatch,
53–55
Competitors, 167
Composite role model, 147
Connections making with
networking,
123–124
Conscious incompetence, 12
Contribution, commercial
about, 167–168
Conversation, 59, 103
appraisal, 185–186
networking, 130–133
at work, 125–127
Credibility, 174
Cross selling
firm's services, 178
work, 178

Delegation, 28–29
Development file, 18–19, 26,
65
Developmental network, 136,
143
Diary, 23
finding energy boosting
slots in, 23–25
as tool, 27–28
Disclosure, 102
Driving force, 109
Due diligence, 154–155

Energy
    boosting slots in diary,
        23–25
    success from, 19–22
Equality, 5
Equilibrium, 151, 152–153
    advice from partners to
        women in their
        firm, 159–161
    due diligence, 154–155
    information from firm,
        155
    my challenges to you, 158
    successful partner,
        153–154
    type of leader, 155–158
Events, networking,
    127–130
Excellent work production,
    102
External maps, 123

Farming, 178–179
Feedback, 63, 69, 184
    advice from partners to
        women in their
        firm, 71
    importance, 65–66,
        68–69
    my challenges to you,
        70–71
    simple model for
        attributable
        feedback, 67–68
    specific, 69
    types, 66–67
Female partners, 2–4, 145,
    148
Financial contribution, 164,
    165
Firm, 39

advice from partners to
    women in their
    firm, 14, 37, 44, 61,
    71, 93–94,
    103–104, 115,
    134, 143–144,
    149, 159–161,
    169, 181–182,
    191, 206–207
business development
    specialists, 179
information from, 155
relationship, 190–191
Focus, success getting from,
    16–18
Framing, 102

Gravitas, 5
Group discussions tips, 205

Human brain, 15
    assumptions and
        stereotypes, 36
    checklist, 15–16
    committing vital
        information to
        memory, 35–36
    components, 33–34
    development file, 18–19
    success getting from focus,
        16–18
    tasks when to do, 34–35
    'to do' lists, 16–18
Human Resources functions,
    167
Hunting, 178–179

Impression management, 81,
    83–84
    advice from partners to
        women in their
        firm, 93–94

BEST, 88–89
binary choice, 81–83
choice, 87
exercises, 86
importance, 84–85
information, 92
my challenges to you, 93
opportunities, 88–90
partners, 91
perception others, 87–88
Individual, 4–6
Inept asses, politics, 99–100
Informal process, 194
Information, 10, 18, 92
    committing vital
        information to
        memory, 35–36
    from firm, 155
    sources of, 195
    see also Feedback
Innocent lambs, politics, 100
Internal maps, 123–124
Intimacy, 175

Leader, 148, 155–158
Limbic system, 33
LinkedIn, 92, 128

'Male orientated' relationship
    building events,
    177–178
Memory, committing vital
    information to,
    35–36
Mental capacity, success
    getting from, 32
Mentors, 137–138
Meritocracy, 2, 3

Neocortex, 33
Network(ing), 117–118, 133

advice from partners to
    women in their
    firm, 134
carving out precious time
    to, 120
conversations, 130–133
events, 127–130
everyday conversations at
    work, 125–127
external maps, 125
within firm, 178
goals, 120–123
internal maps, 123–124
making connections, 123
my challenges to you, 133
opportunities to, 125
people in, 120
at work, 118

Official process, 194
Organisation(al), 4–6
    detritus, 108
    dusting, 107

Paperwork preparation,
    199–201
Partner(s), 88, 91, 95–96,
    153–154, 163
    appraising, 136
Pay, commercial about,
    167–168
Planning, recurring time to,
    25–27
Playing field analysis, 1, 96
    female partners, 2–4
    individual vs. organisation
        vs. society, 4–6
Politics, 95, 96
    advice from partners to
        women in their
        firm, 103–104
    challenges, 103

clever foxes, 99
inept asses, 99–100
innocent lambs, 100
political map, 96–97
professional service firms, 95
using map, 101–103
wise owls, 101
Practice, 11–13, 43, 59, 60
Prefrontal cortex, 33–34
Productive relationships with clients, 175–177
Professional service firms, 1, 2, 5, 9, 16, 27, 95, 194, 198
female partners, 2–4
individual *vs.* organisation *vs.* society, 4–6
Promotion process preparation
advice from partners to women in their firm, 206–207
assessments, 201–204
case studies, 205
group discussions tips, 205
mobilising support, 195–199
my challenges to you, 206
paperwork preparation, 199–201
processing procedures, 194–195

Reliability, 174
Reputational contribution, 164
Role models, 145, 146
advice from partners to women in their firm, 149
composite role model, 147

lack of role models, 145–146
leader, 148
my challenges to you, 149
women assessing other women, 148–149

Selection process, 194
Self orientation, 175
Senior role in professional service firm, 153
Seven Habits of Highly Successful People, 16
Skill, 43
Society, 4–6
Specialist expertise, 29–31
Specific feedback, 69
Sponsor(ship), 138–140
advice from partners to women in their firm, 143–144
appraising partner, 136
challenging for women, 141–142
developmental network, 136
mentors, 137–138
mixed roles, 141
my challenges to you, 143
roles in development, 140
sponsor, 138–140
supporters, 137
tips, 142–143
Stephen Covey's four box model, 16–17
Stepping forward, 105
advice from partners to women in their firm, 115
exercise, 113–114
high fliers, 106

hurdles women to
   navigating way
   around before,
   107–111
my challenges to you, 114
steps, 111–113
Stereotypes, 36, 178–179
Strengths/Weaknesses/
   Opportunities/
   Threats (SWOT),
   73–80
Success
   delegation, 28–29
   getting from energy,
      19–22
   getting from focus, 16–18
   getting from mental
      capacity, 32
   getting from others, 28
   getting from time, 23–28
   identifying and using
      support network,
      31–32
   specialist expertise, 29–31
Supporters, 137

Taking stock, 73
   challenges, 80
   opportunities, 77–78
   strengths, 75–76
   threats, 78
   weaknesses/development
      areas, 76
Thinking, recurring time to,
   25–27
Time
   advice from partners to
      women in their
      firm, 191
   assumptions and
      stereotypes, 36
   checklist, 15–16

committing vital
   information to
   memory, 35–36
development file,
   18–19
diary as tool,
   27–28
finding energy boosting
   slots in diary,
   23–25
human brain, 15
my challenges to you,
   36–37
recurring time to thinking
   and planning,
   25–27
tasks, 34–35
'to do' lists, 16–18
Trust equation, 174–175

Unconscious bias, 5
Unique selling proposition
   (USP), 83

Value, commercial about,
   166–167

Wise owls, politics, 101
Women, 9, 164, 171
   achievements, 184–185
   advice from partners to
      women in their
      firm, 14, 37, 44, 61,
      71, 93–94,
      103–104, 115,
      134, 143–144,
      149, 159–161,
      169, 181–182,
      191, 206–207
   assessing other women,
      148–149
Work/life balance, 46